"Dr. Gary L. McIntosh is a coach who knows the fundamentals of church life and outreach. Every sport requires excellence with athletic fundamentals. All great ball players can throw and catch. When it comes to congregational outreach the fundamentals are inviting, welcoming, and following up with guests. *Beyond the First Visit* is an essential training tool on how to implement these fundamentals."

Dr. John W. Ellas, Center for Church Growth

"Most churches evaluate themselves from the insider's perspective. Gary McIntosh has learned, as a church consultant with years of experience, to see the churches he visits from the first time guest's point of view. . . . We only have one chance to make a first impression!"

Eddie Gibbs, Fuller Theological Seminary

"Gary McIntosh's new book fills a long-standing void. No one (to my knowledge) since Lyle Schaller's *Assimilating New Members*, published in 1978, has addressed the challenge of effectively including new people in the church's life with this much background, savvy, and precision. This book will enable tens of thousands of churches to develop a game plan for reaching, welcoming, including, and developing new people in the local church's life."

George G. Hunter III, distinguished professor of Evangelism and Church Growth, Asbury Theological Seminary

"This book is great! It's filled with practical ideas to tackle every local church's greatest challenge: how to connect and disciple new people. We have already begun to implement many of Gary's excellent ideas."

Dr. Gary D. Kinnaman, author and senior pastor, Word of Grace, Mesa, AZ

Other books by Gary L. McIntosh

Church That Works
Biblical Church Growth
The Exodus Principle
Look Back, Leap Forward
Make Room for the Boom . . . or Bust
One Church, Four Generations
One Size Doesn't Fit All
Staff Your Church for Growth
Evaluating the Church Growth Movement

With Glen Martin
Creating Community
Finding Them, Keeping Them
The Issachar Factor

With Robert Edmondson
It Only Hurts on Monday

With Sam Rima
Overcoming the Dark Side of Leadership

With R. Daniel Reeves
Thriving Churches in the Twenty-first Century

BEYOND THE
FIRST
VISIT

THE COMPLETE GUIDE
TO CONNECTING
GUESTS TO YOUR CHURCH

GARY L. McINTOSH

BakerBooks
Grand Rapids, Michigan

© 2006 by Gary L. McIntosh

Published by Baker Books
a division of Baker Publishing Group
P.O. Box 6287, Grand Rapids, MI 49516-6287
www.bakerbooks.com

Printed in the United States of America

Library of Congress Cataloging-in-Publication Data
McIntosh, Gary, 1947–
    Beyond the first visit : the complete guide to connecting guests to your church / Gary L. McIntosh.
        p.   cm.
    Includes bibliographical references (p.   ).
    ISBN 10: 0-8010-9184-5 (pbk.)
    ISBN 978-0-8010-9184-1 (pbk.)
    1. Church attendance. 2. Church growth. 3. Church marketing. 4. Church work. 5. Hospitality—Religious aspects—Christianity. I. Title.
BV652.S.M35 2006
254′.5—dc22   2006010300

Scripture is taken from the New American Standard Bible—Updated Edition, © 1999 by The Zondervan Corporation; © the Lockman Foundation 1960, 1962, 1963, 1968, 1971, 1972, 1973, 1975, 1977, 1995.

Portions of this book are reprinted from *The Exodus Principle* (Broadman and Holman, 1995) by Gary L. McIntosh. Used by permission.

CONTENTS

1

Empty the Cat Litter Box

I have felt lonely, forgotten or even left out,
set apart from the rest of the world.
I never wanted out. If anything I wanted in.

Arthur Jackson

Whenever company is coming over to our house, my family goes through a regular ritual called "getting ready for company." For us it involves such things as cleaning the bathrooms, emptying the trash cans, vacuuming the floors, dusting the counters, and, most important, changing the cat litter boxes. All our effort is expended in preparation for our guests. We want our house to look the best, and we spare no amount of effort to see that it is ready. No doubt you can identify with this experience.

Growing churches also spend a significant amount of time getting ready for their company—visitors. For them it involves such things as preparing an attractive worship service, organizing teams of greeters, cleaning the church facility, offering refreshing snacks,

7

and, most important, creating a welcoming environment. These churches believe they have only one chance to make a first impression, and they want the visitor to experience a friendly welcome.

We're a Friendly Church

If you were to survey churches and ask them to list their strengths, almost every one would include, "We're a friendly church." I know this for a fact as I have asked this question of more than one thousand churches during the last twenty-five years. It's interesting that in every one of the churches I coached, someone either wrote on a survey or stated verbally that they believed their church to be a friendly place. It did not matter if the individuals were attending churches in danger of closing down, in the midst of twenty-year-long plateaus, or bursting forth in growth. They all felt their church was a friendly one. Apparently, regardless of the state of their health or their size, most churches consider themselves to be friendly.

However, if you were to have surveyed the visitors who attended those same churches, you might have been given an opposite perception. For example, in one church I consulted with a few years ago, I discovered that during a two-year period only 3 visitors out of 197 had chosen to remain in the church. Apparently, more than 97 percent of that church's visitors did not feel very welcomed.

Often church visitors report that churches are cold, unwelcoming, and not very friendly. How is it that two people can experience the same event and feel so differently about it? How can members believe their church is friendly, while newcomers experience an unfriendly atmosphere? The answer is perception. Here is how it works. People who attend a church regularly look at the issue of friendliness from the inside out. From their perspective, they are experiencing a friendly atmosphere. They know other people and other people know them—by name. When they have a personal need, their friends take notice and respond with appropriate action. Their perception is that the church is a friendly place.

In contrast, visitors view the issue of friendliness from the outside in. They are experiencing a totally new atmosphere. They may not know other people and other people may not know them. If they have needs, they are rarely noticed, let alone responded to with appropriate action. So visitors may perceive the church as an unfriendly place.

If guests to our church don't think we're friendly, we aren't.

THINK ABOUT IT

Such different perceptions remind us that beauty is in the eye of the beholder or, in this case, friendliness is in the eye of the beholder. Another way to say it is *perception is reality.* We may think our church is friendly, but it is only friendly to the degree that those visiting our church perceive it to be so.

Now, we know that beauty is not always only in the eye of the beholder, nor is perception always reality. For example, some people perceive there is no God, while in reality there is one. As Psalm 14:1 reminds us: "The fool has said in his heart, 'There is no God.'" In a similar way it is possible for a church to be a friendly place even though some visitors perceive otherwise. But this does not change the fact that in the "eye of the beholder," in this case the visitor, perception will be their reality. The bottom line is if visitors do not perceive us as friendly, we are not.

A clear example of this is painfully close to my heart. My mother and grandmother were raised, committed themselves to the Lord, and attended church in Missouri and Oklahoma in the early to mid-1900s. They were loyal to church, like most people of their generations, attending every time the doors of the church were open. After a fire destroyed their apartment in Tulsa, Oklahoma, they moved to Colorado Springs, Colorado, to live closer to my uncle. They found jobs, rented a small house, and went looking for a church.

As I remember the story, their experience was far from positive. They met unfriendly people in every church they attended. Their perception was that churches in Colorado Springs rejected them due to their Okie mannerisms. In reality, I know that not every church they attended was so unfriendly. However, in the eyes of my mother and grandmother the churches they visited were unfriendly, and that was reality as far as they were concerned. Their perception was strong enough that my mother, who was twenty-four at the time, and my grandmother, who was fifty-one, never attended any church on a regular basis for the rest of their lives.

The point is we must get ready for company! Company's coming to our church every Sunday, and what visitors perceive in our welcome will influence their feelings and response to church and the Lord for years to come. Their viewpoints and perceptions must be considered valuable. What do visitors think about our church? How friendly do they perceive us to be? What steps can we take to welcome them better than we presently do? We must learn to attract, welcome, and follow up on guests so that they stay!

Our Welcoming God

Wanting to welcome newcomers to our church is more than a misguided attempt at consumer marketing. It is simply following the example set by God, who instructed Israel, "When a stranger resides with you in your land, you shall not do him wrong. The stranger who resides with you shall be to you as the native among you, and you shall love him as yourself, for you were aliens in the land of Egypt; I am the LORD your God" (Lev. 19:33–34).

In the Old Testament, strangers were people of foreign blood, who wanted to live among the Israelites. Being outsiders and aliens, strangers did not normally enjoy the rights possessed by the residents of the country they visited. God instructed Israel, however, to welcome strangers, do them no wrong, and love them as members of the family. In practical terms strangers were allowed to listen to the reading of the law (Deut. 31:12); celebrate festivals, such as the Feast of the Atonement (Lev. 16:29) and the Feast of Booths (Deut. 16:14); and participate in religious observances (Num. 19:10). Outsiders enjoyed most of the same rights as native Israelites, such as freedom from oppression (Exod. 22:21), access to physical care (Lev. 19:10), and legal protection (Deut. 1:16; 24:17; 27:19). They also worked in building the temple (1 Chron. 22:2) and served in the army (2 Sam. 1:13).

The reason God required Israel to welcome strangers was the nation's experience in Egypt. "For you also were strangers in the land of Egypt," God explained. If anyone understood what it was like to be an oppressed outsider, it was Israel. "You shall not oppress a stranger," God commanded, "since you yourselves know the feelings of a stranger, for you also were strangers in the land of Egypt" (Exod. 23:9; see Gen. 15:13). Thus Israel was to treat strangers with the love, protection, and respect they had wished for while living as outsiders in Egypt for four hundred years.

Jesus modeled the welcoming nature of God by accepting sinners. Luke describes one incident when Jesus tried to get away from the people to rest: "the crowds were aware of this and followed Him; and *welcoming them*, He began speaking to them about the kingdom of God and curing those who had need of healing" (Luke 9:11). Later, as tax collectors came to listen to Jesus teaching, the Pharisees and scribes criticized him for welcoming sinners (Luke 15:1–2).

Several different Greek words are used for "welcome" in the New Testament, but used together they suggest the meaning of gladly welcoming someone to one's home as a guest. At the conclusion of Acts, Luke illustrates this aspect of welcoming visitors when he comments regarding Paul's practice: "He stayed two full years in his own rented quarters and was *welcoming all* who came to him" (Acts 28:30). Paul's practice of hospitality is instructive, for *hospitality* means literally "love of strangers." In the New Testament, *hospitality* refers primarily to gracious acceptance of and service to fellow believers (see Rom. 12:13; 1 Pet. 4:9). Yet we must not lose sight of the inherent implications for unbelievers also.

> When we extend our hand of welcome to visitors, we are extending God's hand of grace.

THINK ABOUT IT

Getting ready for company is much more than a sociological process for welcoming newcomers. It is a theological demonstration of God's grace. As God's people, *we are to be welcomers just as God is a welcomer.* When we welcome newcomers to church, we are demonstrating the gracious love and care of God himself. This may be good and well when welcoming those who are already believers, but what if they are unbelievers? Receiving strangers into our church does not mean that we approve of their sin but that we offer acceptance of each person without reserve. As the nation of Israel remembered their own captivity in Egypt, we must remember what it was like when we were captives of sin. Someone welcomed each of us to church and to God while we were yet sinners (see Rom. 5:8). Thus when we extend a hand of welcome to visitors—believers and unbelievers—we are extending God's hand. And at a deeper

12

level, when we welcome visitors, we open the possibility that they will welcome God into their lives. For just as Zacchaeus welcomed Jesus into his home and accepted God's salvation (Luke 19:5–10), the unbelieving visitors we welcome may also welcome God's salvation into their lives.

Guest or Visitor

I suggest that we begin getting ready for company by eliminating the term *visitor* from our church vocabulary. In its place let's insert the term *guest*. Doing this is much more than some foolish policy of political correctness. Each term brings to mind different images, and how we imagine newcomers affects how we will treat them.

For instance, if you were to visit me in California by showing up uninvited at my front door, I would answer your knock with a polite but awkward, "It's good to see you." Of course, what I would really be thinking is, *What are you doing here?* I might even invite you inside, offer you a small snack, and graciously spend some time talking with you. Yet our time together would be somewhat strained since I did not know you were coming and was not able to adequately prepare for you. After a brief visit, I would expect you to leave. As some people say, "Good food, good talk, good night!"

However, if I invited you to be my guest, things would work out quite differently. I would answer your knock with an enthusiastic, "Hi! I was looking forward to seeing you." Once inside, you would find that I had cleaned the house in preparation for your visit, and not only that but my wife had prepared your favorite meal. After an extended conversation, I would invite you to spend the night in our "guest" room. The next day as you started to leave, I would walk you to your car and say, "It was a good time. Please come back soon."

There is a difference between being a visitor—in the first scenario—and being a guest—in the second. Visitors are often unwanted; guests are expected. Visitors just show up; guests are invited. Visitors are expected to leave; guests are expected to stay. Visitors come one time; guests return again. I suggest you begin to change your vocabulary. It will make a difference.

Instinctively we expect churches to be friendly places. Research studies completed by Dr. Win Arn and Dr. Charles Arn in the mid-1980s found a direct correlation between friendliness and potential growth. In short, they found that friendly churches had great potential for growth, while less friendly churches had little potential for growth.[1] True friendliness begins with welcoming newcomers to our church as honored guests.

While no one unites with a church without first visiting, we must remember that connecting guests to our church is a process that goes beyond the first visit. We want to provide a warm and friendly welcome to first-time guests, but it takes more than friendliness to help newcomers connect at a deeper level. *Beyond the First Visit* is a guide to help you develop a complete process for welcoming and connecting guests to your church so that they *stay!*

How to Use Ideas from This Book

Merely reading this book will do you little good. Knowing information or having knowledge is of little value until it finds its way into your church's actions.

To get the most from this book, as you read each chapter, make notes in the margin of the book, scribbling your thoughts and ideas. Then make a list of action steps that you want your church to take during the next year to get ready for company.

Put your action steps on note cards and carry them with you. As each action step is accomplished, scratch it off your list. Read your list every day until all the action steps have been completed.

As each action step is completed, you will find that your church is getting ready for company in ways that touch the lives and hearts of your members, as well as those of your guests.

So find a pen or pencil, and let's get ready for company.

Questions to Ask and Answer

1. What do guests think about your church?
2. How friendly do they perceive you to be?
3. What steps can you take to welcome them better than you do presently?

2

BE A GREAT HOST

Let all guests who arrive be received like Christ. For he is going to say, "I came as a guest, and you received me."

Rule of St. Benedict

Have you been a guest in someone's home and remembered it for years to come? The food was perfect, the friends were warm, and the music was relaxing. Or perhaps you attended a church where the time flew so quickly that you did not even want the service to end. A good host makes a difference, whether you are visiting a home or a church.

What does it take to be a good host and welcome guests in a manner that will increase their desire to return? Whether your church is fifty people or five hundred or five thousand, you have many responsibilities that must be attended to for your guests to feel welcomed. You must draw up a list and send out invitations. You must decide where people will park, how to direct them to the proper entrance, who will greet them as they arrive, and how to point out important locations, such as the restrooms. In addition, someone must determine where people will sit, what to prepare for refreshments, and the appropriate music. The list of details can seem endless. Here are seven ways to be a great host:

1. Invite your guests with a personal invitation.
2. Arrive early to make sure everything is ready for the guests' arrival.
3. Greet the guests warmly at the entrance and escort them to their seats.
4. Assist guests in understanding what is taking place.
5. Anticipate and answer as many questions as possible in advance, so guests do not have to ask.
6. Do something extra to make your guests' visit special.
7. Walk guests to the door and invite them back.

Want to have a productive day? Take a legal pad, sit down for an hour, and work your way through each of the seven ways to be a great host listed above. Write each statement by number, leaving five to ten lines under each one. Then make a list for each one, noting every way your church presently accomplishes that aspect of being a good host. When you are finished, go back with a different color pen and write a second list of new or additional ways to fulfill each area. Once you have completed this on your own, consider working through the list with appropriate groups in your church. Not only will you assess your current success in being a great host, but also you will challenge yourself to be even better in the days ahead.

Getting ready for company requires us to think of ourselves as hosts and of those who visit us as our guests. This seems too obvious to even mention, but sometimes the simple ideas are the ones we forget. So as we prepare to be great hosts, let's remember several facts that have been discovered over the years about welcoming guests to church.

Planning Required

Welcoming guests does not happen by accident or even naturally. Churches that sit back and expect new people to find their way into the church's networks of friendships and participants are going to be disappointed. In most churches the social and service networks are closed to the natural addition of new people. So new people simply cannot find their way in. Of course, there are some people who work their way into the life and ministry of a church. For example, if you do not invite highly gregarious people out for dinner, they invite you. If you do not shake their hand, they shake yours. Unfortunately, very few newcomers are highly gregarious. The average guest simply does not have the desire or personality to fight his or her way into the social networks of the church.

> Welcoming guests does not happen accidentally.

THINK ABOUT IT

The Church's Responsibility

Helping guests feel welcomed is the responsibility of the church not the guests. When people enter a new environment, they must be introduced to its culture. In factories and other types of businesses, this orientation takes place through formal training. New workers attend classes to learn about the history, expectations, and requirements of the company. A long-term employee often takes new hires on a tour of the facilities and introduces them to other workers they meet along the way.

The company takes the responsibility to welcome new employees and guide them in discovering the various ins and outs of company culture. Likewise, growing churches do not expect guests to find their way alone through the maze of relationships and expectations of their church. Healthy churches take responsibility for welcoming guests, which includes helping new people understand and become involved in the life of the church.

Growth through Guests

It takes guests to grow. People do not become committed members of a church without first visiting the worship service and other ministries. Unfortunately, most churches are seeing fewer guests coming. This is due to numerous changes in our culture. For example, with the improvements in automobiles and roads following World War II, North Americans grew even stronger in their love affair with the car. Families still fit the "breadwinner and homemaker" nuclear family format of father, mother, and 2.2 children. A pastor looking out his office window in the early 1950s would have counted three or four people in every car driving into the church parking lot.

Today a pastor viewing cars out the same window will most often see only one or two people in each car. Each family unit is about half the size of the 1950s' family, and each car brings about 50 percent fewer people to church. Because fewer people are visiting, each guest arriving at our church is more valuable. We must be more effective in welcoming those who do take the initiative to visit. If our churches are going to grow, we must become better hosts.

The Habit of Overlooking Guests

Churches often overlook new people. A few years back my wife and I visited a church for a few months. The men of the church played in the city's fast-pitch softball league during the fall of the year. Since I have played baseball and softball most of my life, it would have been a natural way for the church to welcome me into the life of the church. However, the first I even heard of the softball team was when an announcement was made from the pulpit that the softball team had recently forfeited two games because not enough players showed up. Players were encouraged to make the games a priority, but no invitation was given to new people to come out for the team.

This overlooking of newcomers also showed up in other ways. Each week the pastor played the piano for the worship service, after which he stepped to the pulpit to give the announcements, then returned to the piano to play the offertory. He then preached the sermon, and then walked back to the piano to play the invitation hymn. Newcomers to the church who were very capable of assisting in the music ministry were never asked to serve. The church simply overlooked them. Stories like this can be told about most churches today.

Helping Guests Fit In

People no longer come to church simply because it is the thing to do. Even when they do visit, well-worn methods of follow-up are not as effective as they once were in getting people to return, let alone become regular worshipers.

Just a little more than fifty years ago, approximately 90 percent of a church's guests came from the same denominational background. This meant that they already understood the church's theology, order of worship, music, values, and culture. Such inherent knowledge allowed them to feel comfortable and at ease in the church. We would have had little need to explain anything in a church of the 1950s. Most newcomers knew how to fit in the church.

In today's world only 30 percent of our guests will come from a sister church or one of a similar background. That means that 70 percent come with little or no understanding of our church. When nearly three-fourths of our guests arrive either with no church background or from a church that is quite different, there is a corresponding lack of knowledge about our church. Many guests will not be familiar with our worship format. They will not know when to stand, sit, or kneel. Others will not know our songs, language, and religious jargon. They will not know how to fit in or get involved in ministry. Therefore, we must be intentional in developing effective ways to move guests beyond the first visit if our churches are to thrive.

Front-Door and Side-Door Churches

Churches have doors through which people enter and exit. Some churches are front-door churches, others are side-door churches, and a very few are multiple-door churches. All churches have back doors—ways people leave a church.

About 90 percent of churches in the United States are front-door churches. This means that most of the new people who connect with the church will make first contact through the worship service, rather than through small groups or other ministries. Churches that focus primarily on front-door ministry must put major emphasis on being effective hosts.

Being a healthy, growing front-door church requires:

- effective ways to invite people to church
- a worship service that is well presented
- a pastor who is an above-average preacher
- workable systems for welcoming newcomers
- clear pathways for becoming involved in membership and/or ministry

Front-Door Church

Newcomers enter through the worship services.

Only about 10 percent of churches in the United States are side-door churches. In a side-door church, most of the new people who connect with the church make first contact through a ministry other than the worship service, for example, through small groups, adult classes, and other types of ministries. Being a healthy side-door church requires:

- a high value on evangelism and meeting people's needs
- effective ways to invite newcomers to the various groups and classes offered by the church
- a well-designed and functional small-group ministry
- a pastor who has an above-average ability to delegate responsibilities

Side-Door Church

Self-Help Groups

Bible Study

Sports Team

Fellowship Group

Care Group

Accountability Group

Newcomers enter through
various groups or classes.

- laypeople committed to caring for those outside the church

A few churches combine both front-door and side-door ministries effectively. Often such churches explode in growth (numerical and spiritual) due to the numerous ways people are invited, welcomed, and involved in church ministry.[1]

A Mobile Society

In our society today there is a continuous process of people entering and leaving the church. Technically, this is called people-flow, and people tend to flow into and out of churches in a regular pattern. Each church is different, but today the average church loses about 10 percent of its worshipers each year (some many more).

In the early 1950s people stayed longer in churches. The best guess is that in those times churches lost only about 5 percent of their people each year. Family units were still intact and neighborhoods and mutual networks of friendships were fairly strong. The general culture supported a friendliness that benefited churches, giving them a natural openness that made all who came feel welcome. This, coupled with the tendency of people to remain in the same geographical area and in the same job for a lifetime, meant that welcoming guests was not a major concern for churches.

Today our mobile society finds people moving three to six times, with some moving up to twenty times, during their lifetime. Add to this the fracturing of the family and the breakdown of natural networks of friendships, and we can see that it is more of a challenge to welcome guests today.

Rates of Retention

Welcoming people is a never-ending process. Research completed in the late 1980s found that a church must keep about 16 percent of its first-time guests to experience a minimal growth rate of 5 percent a year.[2] Rapidly growing churches keep between 25 and 30 percent of their first-time guests. Declining churches keep only about 5 to 8 percent of their first-time guests. By using the average of 16 percent, we can calculate the number of guests our church needs to grow. As an example, a church that wants to add fifty new members this year will need to have a minimum of three hundred guests attend its worship services during the year.

The same research revealed the crucial importance of getting guests to return for a second visit. A church keeps about 85 percent of its guests who come back for a second visit the week after their first visit. This points out the importance of being gracious hosts the first time, so that our guests will feel encouraged to return.

The Importance of Relationships

When people make friends, become involved in a group, and find a place to serve, they will remain in a church. People stay in churches primarily because of relationships. Research has demonstrated that newcomers who remain in a church more than six months have an average of seven friends in their church, while people who drop out of a church average only two friends.[3]

A church keeps about 85 percent of its guests who come back for a second visit the week after their first visit.

As new people come into a church, new small groups must be formed. Friendships develop when people gather together in groups, particularly when the group is working toward a

THINK ABOUT IT

common purpose. Groups normally close quickly to the addition of new people, making it crucial that churches keep starting new groups.

Not only do great hosts help their guests feel welcome, but they introduce new people to new friends and help them find a place of involvement in group settings.[4]

A Science and an Art

Welcoming people is a science and an art. While there are principles and practices that can be followed to help churches be better hosts, welcoming guests so that they stay is more than applying scientific methods. The healthiest churches are intentional about welcoming people, but becoming members of a church is not the same as fitting in or belonging. At the root of being a great host is faith that God will welcome the newcomer into our midst as we put into practice well-designed strategies and plans.

Questions to Ask and Answer

1. How good are you at being great hosts to your guests?
2. Is your church best described as a front-door or side-door church? What implications does this have for welcoming guests?
3. Which of the ten principles found in this chapter do you see operating in your church?

3

SEE WHAT VISITORS SEE

You never have a second chance to make a first impression.

Anonymous

I was visiting a church in Indiana. As I walked into the church lobby, the person who was walking with me commented, "You'll like our church. It's a very friendly place."

Once inside the building, we were immediately met by a man carrying an armful of papers. Introductions were made, he was polite, and we shook hands. However, it was what followed that surprised me.

On completing our handshake, the man turned to my friend and began to talk about some church business that, in truth, should not have been discussed in my presence.

As they talked, the man moved nervously, shifting from one foot to the other, gradually moving so that within a few minutes his back was to me.

I remember thinking, *Hey! I'm the guest here. Quit ignoring me!* But I didn't say anything.

Once he was finished discussing his bit of church business, he seemed to catch a glimpse of me in his peripheral vision. In an embarrassed and hasty attempt to make me feel welcome, he turned toward me and said, "It was nice to meet you. You'll like our church. It's a very friendly place."

The Truth about Encounters

> A moment of truth is any occasion in which a person comes into contact with and forms an impression of your church.
>
> **THINK ABOUT IT**

When a person talks to a member of your church or calls the church on the phone or receives a church brochure in the mail or drives into your parking lot, it is a moment of truth.

A *moment of truth* (MOT) is any occasion in which a person comes into contact with and forms an impression of your church.

Admittedly it is not easy to evaluate the success or quality of these moments of truth. There is little tangible evidence to evaluate, and this is the reason it is so difficult to assess the effectiveness of such encounters. Suffice it to say that the end result of a moment of truth in the life of a guest is a feeling—either positive or negative—about your church. And you want it to be positive.

Before we consider how to describe, analyze, and assess the quality of our guests' experiences during those critical moments of truth, we need to understand the following.

Out of Mind, Out of Sight

Remember that people outside of your church do not go around thinking about you. Those of us who are church leaders tend to spend all day long, sometimes all night long too, with the weight of our church on our heart and mind. Hardly an hour goes by without some thought concerning our church. In many cases we extend our concern for our church to others, thinking unconsciously that others know about and think often about our church also.

Wake up! Such is not the case. People outside your church are bombarded with so much information in our society that most likely they never think of your church—not even once.

I was shocked into this reality while pastoring a church in Southern California a number of years ago. In an effort to greet people and introduce them to our church, we organized a neighborhood canvass. Sixteen of our leaders went door-to-door talking to people and telling them about the ministry of our church. Following each two-hour time period, we would meet back at the church to discuss our experiences. During one such debriefing, one of our elders reported that a neighbor lady had asked where our church was located, mentioning that she had never seen the building. He kindly pointed out our building, which could be seen just down her street. He later discovered that she had lived in her home for ten years. Our church had been on the same street for nearly twenty-three years. Here was a lady who lived only two blocks from our church and did not know we were there!

Now, obviously, during the ten years she had lived in her home, she had driven past our church. The issue was not whether she had seen us, for she clearly could not have missed us. The issue was that she never thought of us. We were never on her mind! It is the opposite of the old saying, "Out of sight, out of mind." For people in our information-saturated society it's "Out of mind, out of sight." Since she did not think of us, she never saw us, even when we were right down the block.

The Importance of Positive Contact

Remember that your church exists in such a person's mind only when he or she makes some type of contact with you, either directly or indirectly.

The lady who lived just down the street from our church knew nothing about our ministries, our people, our child care, or our worship service. The visible picture of our building, landscaping, and sign were not developed in her mind. She did, however, come face-to-face with our church in that brief moment of truth when an elder talked with her in her yard. In that encounter she met our church and made some important evaluations about our leadership and ministry.

People make eleven decisions about us in the first seven seconds of contact.

THINK ABOUT IT

I am not aware of any studies that have been completed on the number of impressions made during moments of truth in relationship to a church. However, one secular report notes that, on average, people make eleven decisions about us in the first seven seconds of contact.[1] There is no doubt that the lady living just down the street from our church was making quick evaluations about our church, impressions that would last for years in her mind. Do not underestimate these moments of truth.

Generalized Impressions

Remember that the impression formed by such contact is generalized in an individual's mind to your entire church. It is sobering to realize that when people outside your congregation develop an impression of your church, based on one moment of truth, their impression will extend to cover your entire church. I had such an experience three years ago.

I was board chairman of a local Christian high school that was looking to relocate to a nicer facility. One day while driving in the north end of town, I went past a church that was in the area of town where we hoped to relocate. The church building appeared large enough to accommodate our school, but what caught my eye in that moment of truth was the number of weeds in the parking lot. Weeds were growing to a height of about three feet, some maybe four feet, out of cracks in the blacktop. On further investigation I found all the gates in the fences locked. Although I could not see through the stained glass windows, the building appeared to be deserted.

Immediately I made my eleven decisions about that church, the most exciting of which was that the church must be closed and possibly for sale. When I arrived home, I began making phone calls, attempting to track down someone with information about this church. It took several weeks but eventually a phone call to the church was answered. I introduced myself and explained that I had driven by the building and it looked so run down, I wondered if it was for sale. My bluntness must have shocked the person I was speaking with, for his response was a classic case of "the silence was deafening." In no uncertain terms he corrected my impressions by informing me that the church was open and not for sale. He wondered how I could ever come to such an illogical conclusion.

My arrival at such an illogical conclusion was actually quite easy. I simply generalized to the entire church my impressions from a single moment of truth. The sad aspect of this encounter was not that the building was unavailable to my Christian school. More crucial was the probability that many people came to the same conclusions I had and drove right on by without visiting.

The End Result

Remember that the end result of any contact is a feeling—positive or negative—about your entire church. Think back to the opening story of this chapter. What do you think I felt about the church I visited in Indiana? As I recall, the worship service was excellent. The Sunday school class I attended kept my attention, and several nice people greeted me. The church buildings were new, clean, and invitingly up-to-date. Yet every time I think about that particular church, I remember that first moment of truth in the lobby. In this case my feeling is neither positive nor negative. Being an experienced church visitor, I am not going to write the church off as unfriendly. In fact I know the opposite to be true. On the other hand, I do not carry a strong positive feeling about the church, simply due to that one, brief moment of truth.

Consider the lady down the street from the church I pastored. What do you think she felt about our church after meeting one of our elders? It is difficult to know, but be sure of this. Whatever she felt in that single moment of truth became her impression of our entire church.

Moments of Truth

Close your eyes and envision a beautiful garden that you may have seen somewhere in your past experience. If you are like me, you do not picture a single flower or plant but an entire garden in full bloom. If an image is not forming clearly, simply picture a single rose. Then picture a dozen roses in a beautiful vase. Finally picture an entire garden of roses. Which picture makes the greatest impact? The single rose, the dozen roses, or the rose garden?

The correct answer is "It depends." At times nothing outshines a display of a dozen roses. The bouquet of roses and baby's breath in a beautiful vase is impressive. At other times the simple gift of a single rose will melt the heart of someone you love. Still, the cumulative effect of an entire rose garden is magnificent.

Such is the possibility of the moments of truth people outside our church may have. A single encounter may be engaging, but in most situations, it is the cumulative effect of several moments of truth that form the most powerful impact. My moment of truth driving by the church with weeds growing in the parking lot was like a single rose. That one impression shaped my view of the church significantly.

My experience with the church in Indianapolis was like a dozen roses displayed in a vase. I had numerous moments of truth, and they formed my picture of the church. Together they lessened the negative impact of the first encounter. At that church, of course, I did not develop a total perception, which could only have come by observing their entire garden—moments of truth with a number of people in various situations.

Thinking of a church in terms of moments of truth creates a powerful tool to help us address and evaluate the quality of our friendliness. It enables us to redirect our thinking from programs to serving those Christ has called us to reach.

By defining the moments of truth that your guests are likely to experience, you can begin to build a church that is indeed friendly and inviting to people on the outside.

There are, of course, innumerable and varied moments of truth. However, guests entering every church encounter certain standard moments of truth. Read through each of the following and think what happens now and what should happen when a guest encounters each moment of truth at your church.

MOT 1: Receiving an Invitation to Church

Not many people visit a church today without receiving some form of invitation. It may come through a personal contact with a friend at work or a neighbor, or it may be a direct-mail piece sent to the home. The common saying "You do not have a second chance to make a first impression" should be taken seriously. First impressions make a greater impact than any other single moment of truth, although the total perception created by several moments of truth may overpower the initial impression.

MOT 2: Driving by the Church Building

For some people this second moment of truth will be their first impression. If your church is located in a high-traffic area, you can be certain that many people are driving by each day. When they drive up to the facility, an additional moment of truth is added to other previous encounters. Among other aspects, they will notice if the landscaping around the church is well kept, if the parking lot is nicely paved and clear of debris, if the exterior walls and windows of the building are attractive, and if there are parking spaces clearly marked for guests.

MOT 3: Walking to the Front Door

For most guests, getting out of their car and walking up to the church building is a major moment of truth. Some start to feel tense as they imagine what they will find inside the church building. Will there be warm and friendly people? Are they entering the building by the proper door? Will they need to ask a lot of embarrassing questions? Are they dressed appropriately?

Some researchers call this newcomer anxiety or "new-turf nerves." Surveys reveal that 75 percent of people say they are more anxious the first time they enter a new place, such as a business, church, or office, than at most other times in their life.[2] This newcomer anxiety creates a heightened sensitivity in new people that causes every experience to make a greater impact on them than the same experiences would make on old-timers in the church.

MOT 4: *Entering the Front Door*

Newcomer anxiety causes new guests to form the bulk of their impressions about a church within thirty seconds of walking in the front door. All the impressions are subconscious, but they are being made quickly nonetheless. Contributing to their subconscious thoughts are such things as sounds, smells, signs, pictures, bulletin boards, colors, lighting, and the general decor.

MOT 5: *Meeting People*

Initial contacts with people play a major role in guests' thoughts about a church. Are church members outgoing and approachable? Do they express an attitude of acceptance? Is there an honest friendliness without being mushy or overbearing? Are friendly people available to answer questions and give assistance? Much of the impact made on guests comes through the body language of people they meet. Simple actions, such as smiling or frowning, leave lasting images on a guest.

MOT 6: Experiencing Ministries and Services

The ministries or amenities explored will obviously vary from guest to guest. Those with small children want to find a child-care area that is clean, bright, open, and safe. Those needing to use the restrooms hope to find them clean and free of unpleasant odors. Those attending a class expect comfortable and nicely decorated classrooms staffed with gracious people.

MOT 7: Entering the Sanctuary

Guests entering the worship area wish to find smiling ushers who have a servant attitude. They expect to be welcomed graciously and treated with respect and to find room to sit without being crowded.

MOT 8: Participating in the Worship Service

The atmosphere of the worship service should be vibrant and happy. Usually guests won't know our church's tradition or practice in worship. Thus they hope to find an order of worship that is easy to understand and follow. They hope to hear songs that are familiar or easy to learn, or they may simply want to be left alone to listen to the music without being forced to participate. Most of all, guests hope to feel at ease and comfortable, and they pray that the worship service will not go too long.

MOT 9: Leaving the Worship Service

Guests trust that on leaving the worship area they will find a friendly atmosphere where they are greeted but not besieged.

Most guests are open to invitations to a refreshment table, where they will meet and talk with people from the church. But they want to feel that they have a choice in staying or leaving. No arm twisting please.

MOT 10: *Being Contacted during the Week*

In our day of cocooning and the necessity of both spouses in many families having to work, it is safe to predict that most guests do not want an unannounced visit to their home. Yet usually they are willing to talk by phone and share their personal feelings about their visit to your church. A gracious invitation to return is more than welcome, as well as a personal letter from the pastor.

MOT 11: *Ongoing Contacts in the Future*

Guests expect to end up on your mailing list to receive appropriate information in the months ahead. Most will appreciate receiving a church newsletter, informational brochures describing ministries they might find interesting, and occasional personal invitations to special events.

In Olympic events, such as ice-skating and gymnastics, which are judged by people watching the performance, an interesting factor comes into play. Many aspects of the performance count in the final score, but the most crucial factors are the beginning and the end. If an Olympic athlete begins well and ends well, then all's well. The implication is that the first and last impressions are the most important on the final score.

This applies to moments of truth as well. The most important moments of truth for a guest are their first and last ones. Be assured that guests have already made many judgments about your church before your pastor even begins to preach. Impressions formed by the first moment of truth are carried along and color to some degree all succeeding encounters. Since the last moment of truth remains freshest in the mind, it supersedes those that fall in between the first and last. The total perception comes into play, but be certain that the first and last moments of truth are extremely powerful.

Questions Guests Ask

When newcomers encounter each of these moments of truth, they ask questions that differ from those of long-term members. The following are four questions guests ask when visiting a church.

Is There Room for Me?

A few weeks ago I was consulting with a church in northern California. During the worship service, I quietly slipped out and walked through the parking lot. While observing the parking situation, two people entered the lot and drove around looking for a parking space. When they could not find a space in which to park, they left. Guests notice if the parking lot is full, or if there is enough seating in the auditorium. If guests do not perceive that there is enough room for them, they leave or do not return for a second visit.

Is There Room for Me Personally?

When guests attend your church, the first thing they do is look around to see if there is anyone else there like them. Newcomers want to know if there are others who may have a similar background, age, or life stage. They hope to find groups of people who have the same interests, and they particularly look for specialty groups that will meet their needs.

Is There Room for Me Relationally?

Guests want more than a friendly church. What they really want are friends. After attending your church for a few weeks, newcomers will notice if members are making room for them in the various classes and/or small groups or if classes are closed off to them.

Is It Worth It?

The demand on people's time in our society is heavy. Once people begin attending a church, they will ask if it is worth their time to attend. Involvement in worship, ministries, classes, and/or groups will be judged on the basis of how each meets their specific needs.

Awareness Tour

Is there room for your guests physically, emotionally, and personally at your church? Will they find it worth the time to attend and participate in your church? An awareness tour is one way to find out.

Church leaders are so familiar with their church that they take for granted how others see and respond to each moment of truth. Taking an awareness tour through the eleven moments of truth given above is a way to see your church through guests' eyes.

To honestly appreciate the new person's experience, you need to set aside your "insider" understanding about your church and think like an "outsider."

1. Start by making a list of the moments of truth discussed in this chapter. Type the headings, leaving two to three inches of space beneath each one. Make a copy for each board member.

2. At your next board meeting, ask each member to leave everything in the boardroom except a pen or pencil and walk with you about a block away from your church.

3. Explain that you want them to pretend they have never been to your church before. Tell them to look at your church through "guest eyes" and jot down what guests see as they encounter each moment of truth listed on the paper you hand out to them.

4. Actually walk through the moments of truth, stopping briefly at each area to allow your leaders to look around and jot down what guests see. At each point they should imagine how the people there would respond to the guest.

5. Complete your tour, return to the boardroom, and discuss the experience, going through the moments of truth from beginning to end. Ask, What do guests see, experience, and feel from these moments of truth in our church? What should they experience? What can our church begin to do to make these moments of truth positive experiences for our guests?

Questions to Ask and Answer

If you were a guest visiting your church . . .

1. Would you be impressed with the facility and landscaping?
2. Would you be able to find the restrooms without asking?

3. Would you feel comfortable leaving your child in the nursery?
4. Would you understand what takes place during the worship service?
5. Would you feel embarrassed or pressured during your visit?
6. Would you be greeted and accepted as you are?
7. Would you come back next week?

4

Notch Up Your Ministry

In a fast food culture you have to remind yourself that some things
cannot be done quickly. Hospitality takes time.

Anonymous Benedictine monk

I observed "the pride factor" in action a few years ago when
my wife and I decided to have our driveway enlarged. The
driveway was adequate when we had only two cars, but after our
boys began driving and purchased their own cars, we just didn't
have enough room. The company we hired to do the job was
owned and operated by two brothers who were both Christians
and committed church members. We had developed a friendship through other contacts, and we ended up talking quite a
bit while the work was in progress.

One day we were engaged in conversation about sports while
waiting for the dump truck to come and pick up the broken pieces
of concrete left over from the demolition of our old driveway.
Casually one of the brothers asked me if I knew of a good church

where he could take a close friend. His question shocked me since I knew he attended a church in our city. Picking up on my surprised expression, he launched into a long discourse about how he loved his present church, his pastor, and the people he had known there for so many years. He was hesitant though about inviting his close friend, who was not a Christian, to attend his church.

Continuing on, he commented that he worshiped at his church due to the friendships he had there but frankly was embarrassed to bring any friends. He realized that his church's facilities, ministries, and specifically the worship service did not have the qualities that attracted newcomers. Quietly he whispered that if he were looking for a new church, he probably wouldn't even consider his present church. His pride factor was low, and it prevented him from bringing his friend to worship at his church.

> People may attend our church out of a sense of commitment but will not bring their friends if their pride factor is low.

Is church growth an extension of happy people? Yes, to some extent. People won't bring their friends to a church where they are not happy.

THINK ABOUT IT

When we first begin to think of welcoming people to church, it is usually the warm fuzzy things that come to mind, like smiling and being polite. Positive attitudes and actions are a necessary part of a growing church. But we can smile all we want; if people do not find they are being served well through our various ministries, they aren't likely to be back anytime soon. Even more crucial, if our regular worshipers don't have pride in our church and ministry, they won't bring their friends.

A Notch Above

To attract and keep guests in your church, it is necessary to develop a culture of service, which can be difficult when the core ministries and facilities of a church are below the standards or expectations of the people you are attempting to reach.

Here's an example. One church I consulted with was located in an extremely hot climate. Most people in the city had air-conditioning in their homes, cars, and at work. If they attended a movie, ate at a restaurant, or visited a doctor's office, they did it all in air-conditioned comfort. Yet, as you might guess, the church was not air-conditioned! The members couldn't see the necessity of spending the money to air-condition their building. If their church had developed a culture of service, they would have known that providing air-conditioning is a way of serving those they were trying to reach with the gospel. The high cost of installing central air-conditioning was part of their sacrificial service to people not yet a part of their church.

As a rule, your church's ministries and facilities need to be a notch above what your constituency expects or even needs. There are always exceptions, but most people lean toward attending a church that is slightly above their socioeconomic position in life. This means, if people live, work, and play in air-conditioning, not only do they expect your church to be air-conditioned, but they expect it to be a notch better than theirs. Parents don't want your child care to be as good as theirs at home: they want it a notch better. Those with super sound systems in their cars and homes will expect your church's sound system to be excellent. Thus it is vitally important to upgrade your ministries as much as feasible to enhance the overall service level of your church.

Core Ministries

Serving people inside and outside your church means that you offer excellence in all areas of ministry. As you seek to upgrade your ministries, you will want to begin by focusing on three core areas: facility, child care, and worship service.

Facility

You should be concerned about your facilities and grounds because they provide an atmosphere for your church. The decor and upkeep of your facilities tell people a lot about your church and your values. Also they send a hidden message that you care and are interested in serving those whom God directs your way. The inherent message in well-designed, decorated, and kept facilities is: "We care about our church and we care about you."

Periodically look at your grounds, buildings, and facilities and ask, "Is there anything we need to change?" Look at it as a visitor would. Does it look inviting? Is it done in good taste? Does the carpet need to be replaced? Is there anything that looks out of date? Is there anything that would cause people to say, "I like that"? You want people to experience a sort of "wow" factor when they drive up or walk into your church building. The furniture, fixtures, lights—every detail—should contribute to making people's visit to your church a pleasant experience. Your church building doesn't have to be elaborate, but it must be attractive and well maintained. People should walk in and say, "Oh!" rather than "Ouch!"

Carefully watch the overall image your church communicates through its colors, style, and decorations. I was asked to visit a church in California that once had been a model for other churches in the southwestern part of the United States. Walking into the sanctuary, a bygone era screamed out to me through the colors of paint and carpet, the styles of drapes and furniture, and the pictures and literature displays.

While observing another church, I noted a musty odor immediately on entering the building. My recommendation to the church leaders of both churches was to hire a professional to advise them on how they could update the atmosphere of their sanctuary. For one church it simply meant removing twenty-five-year-old carpet and installing new padding and carpet to rid its building of a damp, musty smell that had accumulated over the years. The other church faced more extensive remodeling that would take place over a period of three to five years.

Understandably most churches cannot afford to replace furniture and make structural changes to their facilities very often. The expense is prohibitive. Churches ought to plan, however, on redecorating every five years by replacing or upgrading paint, landscaping, signs, fixtures, drapes, and other decorative items that can be changed fairly easily.

At another church the huge education building gave evidence of a large and vibrant Sunday school program. Or at least that was the way it had been nearly ten years before. Now, as the pastor led me on a tour of the church buildings, he was decrying the lack of attendance and asking questions beginning with "Why?" I marked on my list of items to discuss later the narrow hallways, which had been painted purple, and the dark brown carpet, but what really caused me distress were the restrooms. One women's restroom had a lightbulb hanging down about one foot from the ceiling by an electrical cord. In another there was no mirror. In yet another the stench was bad enough that I wouldn't have wanted to use it. After my candid assessment of the restrooms, the church board immediately appropriated the money to remodel them. About six months later, I had the opportunity to visit again. The new carpet, fixtures, lighting, mirrors, and chairs of the remodeled restrooms were very attractive

46

and inviting. To the women who use it now, the restroom makes a positive statement: "We care about you and are here to serve you." What a difference from the previous statement!

Arriving at a church in New Jersey where I was to preach, I parked two blocks away and walked in snow and ice to the front of the building. The sign said "Sanctuary" and pointed to what was obviously the front door. Rushing up the steps, I opened the door, walked through a dark entryway, and entered a second door to find myself standing at the front of the sanctuary with the entire congregation staring directly at me. How embarrassing! Later the pastor explained that the entrance I used had been the front entrance many years before. A remodeling of the building had resulted in the complete reversal of the sanctuary. Now everyone entered through what at one time was the back entrance. There was only one small problem. They hadn't changed the sign! Everyone who attended the church regularly just knew to enter the back door, not the front door. I wondered how many guests had made the same mistake I had. I didn't need to wonder how they felt. I already knew.

> The quality of your church buildings, grounds, and ministries sends a message to people. What message is your church sending?
>
> **THINK ABOUT IT**

There are only three reasons for signs: to name your church, to announce your services, and to give directions. If a sign doesn't do one of these three things, take it down; it is useless. Like other aspects of your facilities, signs communicate your values in a subtle way, so do them right. Make sure signs match. Colors, logos, pictures, and of course, the directions on them should be up-to-date and correct.

Another critical aspect of notching up your facility relates to what is perhaps the best-known principle of church growth — the 80 percent rule. Basically this rule states that when an area, such as an auditorium, becomes 80 percent full, growth begins to decline. This is true for small groups meeting in homes, adults gathering in Bible fellowship classes, or attendees at a worship service.

Why does the 80 percent rule seem to hold up? A number of years ago anthropologist Edward T. Hall conducted a pioneering study on the effects of distance in relationships. He identified four main body-space zones and labeled them *intimate, personal, social,* and *public.*

The *public zone* is the distance at which pastors, teachers, and lecturers most often stand in relation to their audience—about twelve feet or more between speaker and listener. The *social zone* is the distance we often stand apart from each other when talking in a small group. This zone is between four and twelve feet and is suitable for fairly impersonal exchanges, such as in meetings or interviews. The *personal zone* is within the normal touching range of another person, about eighteen inches to four feet. People often attempt to protect their personal zones by placing handbags, coats, or other barriers between themselves and others. The *intimate zone* is the distance needed for embracing. We allow only family members or close friends into this zone. For North Americans and Europeans, any invasion by strangers into this zone causes mental and physical anxiety, irritation, and fear.

When attendance in a worship service or small group exceeds 80 percent capacity, people are forced into an uncomfortably close seating arrangement. The 80 percent rule comes into play because often the *personal* and even the *intimate* zones of worshipers are invaded.

Of course, people will tolerate being in close proximity for a short while, but eventually the tension created through invasion of their personal and intimate zones forces them to avoid the venue, and so the attendance in a worship service, for example, will slide back down as some people attend less often and others depart to relieve the tension. While attendance may exceed 80 percent for a while, it will do so just temporarily before declining.

The exact point at which guests begin to feel uncomfortable is dependent on the location of the church. Churches in rural areas tend to begin plateauing at 70 percent capacity. Evidently, people who live in a rural area appreciate more open space. On the other hand, churches that meet in urban centers, where the population density is greater, may not experience a plateau until the church reaches 90 percent capacity. Generally speaking, however, the following holds true:

- An attendance of less than 20 percent capacity is intolerably empty. Newcomers will feel exposed to the penetrating gazes of church members.
- 20 to 35 percent full is uncomfortably empty. While members may enjoy seeing new people in attendance, the newcomers usually continue to feel conspicuous.
- 35 to 65 percent full is comfortably empty. New people will feel reasonably accepted, without feeling that everyone knows they are a visitor.
- 65 to 80 percent full is comfortably full. At this level of attendance, both newcomers and old-timers experience the most satisfaction.
- 80 to 100 percent full is uncomfortably full. New people feel there is no "open chair" for them and rarely return to worship again.

- More than 100 percent full is intolerably full. While seeing the church so full is exciting, over time the attendance will drop down to below 90 percent.

In the end, people just need more room!

Looking around, it seems like everything is getting bigger. People order Big Gulps, *venti* lattes, all-you-can-eat salads; they purchase 5,000-square-foot homes and drive Humvees. So it should come as no surprise that people expect more room in their seats at church also. Seat-size standards were set in the 1930s' edition of *Architectural Graphic Standards.* This comprehensive guide for building and design listed 18 inches as the minimum seat width and 21 inches as the "ideal." Today architects use 21 inches as the minimum and 24 inches as the ideal.

These newer standards are just beginning to be used. For example, seats on the new trains in Philadelphia now allow 21 inches per person rather than the 18 inches found on older trains. When the Los Angeles Lakers moved from the Great Western Forum to the new Staples Center, they increased the seating size an extra 3.5 inches. Except for bleacher seats, which are still figured at 18 inches per person, the seats at the brand-new Petco Park in San Diego, California, are 19 to 22 inches wide.

Unfortunately, most churches have seats that conform to the older pre–World War II standards. Theater seats found in older churches are often just slightly more than 17 inches wide, while many older churches figured their seating capacity based on 18 inches per person in pews.

The trend is toward wider, more comfortable seating in all public arenas, even on airlines. Using the new seating capacity guidelines, many churches will discover they do not have the capacity listed on their architectural drawings.

Using the new standards, how many people can fit in your worship center? How willing are your members to give up their seats to newcomers? What is the comfort zone in your worship service? How can you begin to notch up your facilities by making seating more comfortable?

Child Care

Anyone who has been around churches for many years realizes that people have higher expectations today than they did years ago. This is true in all areas of our lives. A good example of the rise in expectations can be seen in today's parents, who look for excellence in the child-care ministry of a church.

Good child care has always been a contributing factor in growing churches. Naturally parents are concerned for their children and want to place them in capable hands while they participate in church activities. Our changing lifestyle means that today child care is especially important. Parents approach child care with higher expectations than those of just a few years ago. Not only do parents want the best for their children, but also they are willing to spend the big bucks to get it. Nike, Chanel, Ralph Lauren, Christian Dior, and Guess are among the many big-name designers that have realized this and now produce infant or toddler clothes.

Parents expect your church to be willing to spend money to provide the best for their children. It is not unusual for today's parents to spend fifteen hundred dollars decorating a baby's room and more than five hundred dollars to furnish it with toys. Accordingly parents expect your church's nursery to be comparable to their baby's room at home. Most important, since many parents hire other people to take care of their children during the workday, they are experienced child-care shoppers. Whether they choose to place their children in day-care centers or with in-home care providers, they know how to find quality care. Parents expect your church to provide the same quality care they would find at the best weekday care centers.

When I do church consultations, I try to take a younger person along to assist me. Younger people see things in a church I often miss. On one trip, my son assisted me. We spent an afternoon touring a church's facilities, looking into every room, office, and storage area. Later my son told me, "Dad, I wouldn't put my children in that nursery." His reason? The slats on the cribs were spaced too far apart. The cribs looked fine to me. In fact, they were the same type of crib my son had slept in as a baby—thirty-one years before! That, of course, was the problem. Safety standards for cribs have changed over the years, a fact of which my son was well aware. He was looking at the nursery with a parent's eye, and so will your younger guests.

Your child-care rooms must be clean and up-to-date. Parents will notice. Sanitize your child-care areas weekly. Regularly clean all surfaces, toys, tables, trays, bedding, bibs, and doors. Place used toys in a bin marked for washing and clean them each week. Clean carpets every other month. Clean walls every month. Redecorate every year. Cute animals are always in style. One year it might be dinosaurs, another year ducks. Today you see cows all over the place.

Evaluate the ratio of children to nursery workers. With trained child-care professionals, there should be no more than four infants per worker and no more than five toddlers per worker. If you use volunteer workers, it is best if there are just two infants or four toddlers per worker. Provide a hazard-free environment. Replace broken toys and furniture. Fix peeling paint, protruding nails, leaking plumbing, and lighting problems. Separate toddlers from babies. Use fire alarms and check them on a regular basis. Maintain good ventilation, heating, and air-conditioning.

Develop child-care policies, which contain information on how discipline is handled, procedures in case of sickness or accident, age guidelines, hours of operation, wellness policies, use of volunteers, registration procedures, and a fire escape plan. Provide a copy for all parents and post one near the entrance of all child-care rooms.

As in most other roles, parents like to see the same people in the nursery and other child-care ministries to gain a sense of trust. A high turnover rate of workers keeps children and parents from building relationships with them. Rotate workers as little as possible and train them all. Explain to them how they are a vital link in your plan to help guests move beyond the first visit. Encourage them to see how they fit into the overall philosophy of your church. Require workers to take first aid training and CPR for infants and children. Recruit and hire workers who interact well with children. It's wise to screen all child-care personnel for past history of child abuse.

To evaluate your church nursery, take a tour as if you were a parent leaving your children there for the first time.

1. Would you be impressed with the decorations and furnishings?
2. Would you be pleased with the cleanliness of the carpet, walls, cribs, and toys?
3. Would you find the child-care policies and fire escape plan posted for easy reading?
4. Would there be anything that would make you hesitate or feel uncomfortable about leaving your children there?

5. Would you sense that your church has taken steps to ensure the safety and welfare of your children?

After your tour of the nursery, make a list of what can be done to serve your people better in the next year.

Worship Service

There are four different styles of worship that are popular in the United States today. Some churches enjoy a high church or Episcopal style, in which rituals, formal readings, and church architecture present people with a picture of the majesty of God. Others appreciate a less formal but traditional approach, which maintains a respect for God through its hymns, prayers, and quiet atmosphere. A more contemporary worship style has gained acceptance today. People like the celebrative atmosphere that allows for personal interaction and the use of new technology and forms of communication like drama. Lastly, many people find that a charismatic approach to worship allows them to freely express and communicate their relationship to God in a joyous manner.

The basic principle to remember is that your message is not the sermon; your message is the service. Your entire worship service from beginning to end is sending out a message. Excellent worship services send out a unified message by building the entire worship service around one theme. Once a broad theme has been selected, then each aspect of the service—music, introductions, announcements, Scripture reading, prayers, drama, and sermon—is selected to support the theme.

Design your worship service to keep people alert by involving them in meaningful ways throughout the service. Build in ways for people to participate by allowing for singing, clapping, standing, shaking hands, praying, hugging, talking, laughing, crying, and other ways that would be acceptable to your worshipers. Pay attention to the flow of the service. Ideally once people enter into the worship time, the service should flow with good pace from one element to the next. While there is no need to rush the service, it needs to move along quickly enough to keep people's attention, with little "dead time" when nothing significant takes place. Worshipers should be able to sense a clear flow or progression. Smooth transitions between the various elements of the worship service are key aspects to develop. Incorporating a variety of worship elements, such as drama, interviews, video, a message, a greeting, Scripture reading, offering, and music, maintains everyone's interest and enjoyment.

The message is not the sermon; the message is the service.

THINK ABOUT IT

You'll know your worship service is celebrative when . . .

1. People attend. Celebrative services attract people who come because they want to rather than because they have to.
2. People bring friends. Celebrative services not only attract people but they also cause worshippers to bring their friends.
3. People participate. Celebrative services create an environment where singing, giving, praying and other areas of worship are entered into with enthusiasm.
4. People listen. Celebrative services hold the attention of worshippers throughout the entire time of worship.
5. People grow. Celebrative services challenge individuals to make biblical decisions that affect their daily living.[1]

This type of worship service requires advanced planning. It also helps to recruit a worship team who can creatively plan the worship services. Above all, effective worship services take seriously the mental, spiritual, relational, and emotional nature of the worshipers. While worship services should challenge people mentally, they must also speak to the emotions, spirits, and hearts of the worshipers to be truly celebrative.

Only 1 Percent

It doesn't always take major changes to upgrade your ministries. A few changes can make dramatic improvements. Realistically you can't make big changes all the time, but you can make small improvements and make them continuously.

Pat Riley, former coach of the Los Angeles Lakers, employed the strategy of small improvements and saw the Lakers repeat as world champions. Intuitively he realized that the other teams in the NBA would be working hard during the off-season to improve their game. If the Lakers didn't improve during the off-season, they would have little opportunity to repeat as champions the following year. He challenged each player to try to improve 1 percent in each of five areas during the next season. The five areas were different for each player, depending on his position and predominant skills. Coach Riley's theory suggested that if each player was successful in improving only 1 percent in five different areas, each would raise the level of his game 5 percent. That would mean the entire team of twelve players combined would improve their game 60 percent! His theory worked and the Lakers repeated as champions.

Rarely do world champion teams repeat as champions for a second, third, or fourth year if they don't improve their skills. The same is true of our church ministry. If we don't see small improvements taking place regularly, the quality of our ministries may be heading downward. There is no need to make major improvements all at once. Our challenge is to make small incremental improvements each and every year. Raising the quality of twelve key ministries by only 1 percent amounts to about a 12 percent increase in a year. Doing that for five years in a row would equal a 60 percent improvement.

Questions to Ask and Answer

1. How willing are your worshipers to bring new people to church? Do they feel good about your church and the ministry it provides?
2. What expectations do people have of your church today that are different from a few years ago? How well are you meeting these new expectations?
3. Which of the three core areas mentioned in this chapter is your church's strongest ministry area? Which is the weakest? What needs to be done in the months ahead to strengthen this weak area?

NOTCH UP YOUR KEY MINISTRIES

- Evaluate all your current ministries and make a list of the twelve most important ones to your church and its future.
- Looking over your list, what could you do this year in each area to improve it by only 1 percent? How can you upgrade each area this year so that it will be better next year? Be as specific and practical as possible.
- Once you've made your list, get started. If you accomplish each one, you'll have upgraded your ministries by about 12 percent.
- Plan your upgrades over a three-to-five-year time span. For example, you may need a new sound system in the sanctuary. If you are unable to purchase the entire system this year, at least buy new microphones. Next year purchase the speakers, and so on. By doing this for five years, you will eventually have your new sound system.

5

CREATE A LASTING IMPRESSION

First impressions in the local church are about creating the atmosphere expressed in Jesus' invitation to grace-filled community in Matthew 11:27–30.

Mark Waltz

Good doctrine, good fellowship, good prayer, and good ministry. Do they guarantee a church will welcome newcomers well? Not necessarily. Sometimes churches do not do well, even though they have the basic ingredients for success.

One problem is that often they are not communicating well to their target audience. Potential guests do not clearly understand "who" and "what" the church is. It lacks image.

Image is an intangible but important part of a church's growth strategy. All the visual symbols of a church—logos, signs, letterheads, advertisements, and facilities—come together to form one unified picture. How is an image created? One way is through advertising. Webster's *New World Dictionary* offers as one definition for image: "impression by the general public, often one deliberately created or modified by publicity, advertising."

Not long ago pastors and church leaders refused to use mass media. The unscrupulous Madison Avenue portrait made advertising techniques appear immoral or manipulative. Today many churches and leaders are using direct mail, the Internet, and newspaper advertising in an effort to communicate their ministry to those outside the church. Letting people know that your church is ready to serve them is vital to attracting new guests.

I doubt seriously if any of the New Testament churches had a brochure or direct mail campaign. However, they did create an atmosphere where growth occurred. Often the means they used were what today we would call advertising.

The personal letters of the New Testament are an obvious advertising medium—direct mail in our terms. Luke, John, James, Peter, and Paul all used this tool to communicate their love, care, teachings, and exhortation to people who could not be reached in any other way.

Word-of-mouth advertising was instrumental in reaching unchurched people around Thessalonica. "For the word of the Lord has sounded forth from you," states Paul, "not only in Macedonia and Achaia, but also in every place your faith toward God has gone forth, so that we have no need to say anything" (1 Thess. 1:8).

Actually the Bible was the first printed piece of advertising. Consider the familiar John 3:16: "For God so loved the world, that He gave His only begotten Son, that whoever believes in Him shall not perish, but have eternal life." All the elements of advertising are found in this verse. The product—Jesus Christ; the price—he's free; the promise—eternal life; and it's guaranteed! God was the very first advertiser. The principles of advertising were created by God!

It Will and It Won't

You say you don't advertise? Wrong! You advertise in hundreds of ways every day through your facilities, grounds, signs, and the moments of truth your members experience with their neighbors, friends, and family members. While advertising is one method that can be used to communicate the Good News, it is not just a gimmick that guarantees converts.

- Advertising will not change reality. Once guests visit, they will find out if the experience lives up to the story. False advertising may get people to attend a church service, but only one time.
- Advertising will not convert people. Even though the gospel is a simple story, advertising is too simplistic to give people a full understanding that leads to personal commitment.
- Advertising will not cause personal growth. Growth occurs over time as people learn, apply truth, and experience life. At the most, advertising can help inform a person of an opportunity that will help him or her grow.
- Advertising will not replace personal relationships. Satisfied customers who tell others about a product are the best advertising available. Andrew told Peter. Philip found Nathanael. Cornelius gathered his relatives and close friends. Word of mouth is always the key.

While not a panacea for all church ills, advertising can be a major part of a church-growth mix.

- Advertising will build morale. A positive advertising strategy can raise a member's morale and give him or her a point of reference for inviting others to church.

- Advertising will create a climate for growth. Through advertising, potential guests can learn of the opportunity for a personal and rewarding relationship with the living God and the church's desire to meet their needs. They can learn of a church's openness to new people.

- Advertising will attract guests. Advertising can create an inviting image and communicate specific opportunities, times, dates, and places for involvement.

- Advertising will shape community attitudes. Advertising offers a church the opportunity to tell the community what it wants them to know. Such ideals as a desire to be helpful, assurance of acceptance, the enthusiasm of present members, and the sense of fulfillment Christ brings to life may be communicated through mass media techniques.

> If you think you don't advertise, you're wrong! Your church advertises in hundreds of ways every day through its facilities, grounds, signs, and the transactions its members make with neighbors, friends, and family members.
>
> The question is not, Do you advertise? It's, What are you communicating to others?

THINK ABOUT IT

How to Begin

Every church begins at square one with the ability and the right to tell others about itself. Your church begins by telling others what you stand for, what you will deliver, and how you will do it. People generally believe what you say about yourself, at least until they come to see for themselves. Expectations lead to people's perceptions. Once you establish expectations, your reputation is on the line. People will expect you to live up to what you say about yourself.

Concerned leaders should begin by building a strong commitment to the Great Commission in their church. The energy and cost of developing a solid advertising strategy will find support among those who care deeply about telling their communities about Christ. Without this foundational belief, advertising will be a shortsighted investment bringing limited results.

Determine your ministry area and focus advertising within this limited geographical area for best results. A ministry area is the geographical area from which a church draws most of its worshipers. This can be determined by placing a pin on a map where your church is located. Then add more pins showing where your worshipers live. A visual picture of your prime ministry area will develop. Or you can call the local planning department of your city or county and ask them what the average trip time is in your community—the average time people spend traveling to shop, go to work, or attend church. It usually falls between ten and twenty minutes. Drawing a circle around your church on a map equal to about an average trip time away from your building will give you a fair idea of your ministry area.

Select your target audiences. Direct different strategies to current members, church shoppers, and the unchurched population you are trying to attract. Research the needs, attitudes, and concerns of your target groups.

Develop a communications team of an editor, writer, artist, and photographer, who will produce announcements, brochures, and other publicity pieces. Cultivate positive word-of-mouth communication and fashion an advertising campaign for those outside the church. Regularly communicate through the use of a newsletter within the church. Balance your strategy to focus inward on church members and outward on potential contacts. Invest 5 percent of your total budget per year in a total advertising plan. Don't give up after the first try. A well-developed image unfolds over several years.

Selecting a New Church Name

Saying hello to your community begins with a good church name. Many churches are named after a place, like Main Street Church. Others are named to designate a denominational affiliation, like Faith Baptist Church. Other names, such as Community Bible Church, open broad doors, while some names hold out spiritual ideals, like Church of the Open Door. Many church names present biblical pictures, like Good Shepherd Lutheran Church. Some contain nearly an entire system of theology, like Pillar of Fire Mount Zion Holiness Church of the Straight Gate. A great name can open doors to the unreached community by communicating the desire of the church to be of service to others.

Today many churches are changing their names. To some this is a new concept, but changing a church name is not as new as many people might think. For instance, the vast majority of early Americans were Anglicans. In fact, two-thirds of the signers of the Declaration of Independence were Anglicans, as were George Washington, John Madison, Patrick Henry, Alexander Hamilton, and John Marshall. After the American Revolution, the Anglicans lost their dominant position. Because the Anglican Church was identified with England, thousands of Americans left to become part of the free churches that reflected America's zeal for freedom. Not until the Anglicans renamed themselves the Protestant Episcopal Church were they able to enjoy growth again.

Why Change Your Name?

Why would a church want to change its name? Here are four reasons some are choosing to do so.

> *New location.* When Park Street Church moves to Fifth Avenue, it will need to change its name or suffer a loss of identity. If the name is not changed, there will be increased confusion as new people move into the community and are unaware that Park Street Church is now located on Fifth Avenue.

> *New target.* The First German Baptist Church initially ministered to a primarily German audience. However, over the years the community has changed and a new target audience must be reached. Without a name change, it is unlikely that people of other ethnic descents will even attempt a visit.

> *New identity.* Twenty years ago Broadway Presbyterian Church struggled through difficult times. Many people left and joined other churches in the local area. Broadway is now experiencing love and peace within its membership, yet its previous reputation lives on. A name change is one way the church can clear away the old memories and create a new identity.

New direction. Faith Community Church organized a vision team to redefine its mission, and they decided to set a new direction for the future. Noting that their community has many hurting people, they elected to communicate their new desire to help with a new name—New Hope Community Church.

Seven Guidelines

If you think a new church name might help you connect with people outside your church, here are seven guidelines to think about as you work through the choice.

1. *Choose a name that attracts the unchurched.* One key to reaching the unchurched is to use a church name that is understandable and attractive to them. Consider what unchurched people think about names like Faith, Grace, and others with religious-sounding connotations. Narrow your choice down to five names and then survey people in movie lines, ballparks, shopping malls, and by phone to see what they think of your choices.

2. *Choose a name that sets you apart.* Churches tend to choose similar names. One church realized that its name was like nine others in the same area. Ask yourself what causes your church to stand out. What makes your church unique? How is your church different from other churches with similar names?

3. *Choose a name that is simple to remember.* An unwieldy name must be classified along with a poor location or a run-down facility—each can be eclipsed, but it often takes extraordinary effort to do so. Keep your name short. Don't

try to say too much in your name. One word is best but two or three words are okay.

4. *Choose a name that helps people find your church.* One pastor jokingly said, "It takes Daniel Boone to find our church!" His church, like many, was established in a small, quiet neighborhood, which today is off the beaten path. Help people locate your church by naming it after a street, a local attraction, a physical landmark, or other unique feature.

5. *Choose a name that removes barriers.* Some people remember churches as places with long lists of don'ts. People shouldn't trip over your theology because of what your name suggests. Look at a potential name through unchurched eyes. Ask unchurched people to give you their first response on hearing your new name. Hire a consulting firm to investigate possible new names for you and make a recommendation on which one to select.

6. *Choose a name that expands your potential.* Don't limit your drawing power to one city or geographical area, unless there is tremendous potential for growth in that area. Select a name broad enough to include an entire city rather than simply a neighborhood, a name with regional rather than just city identity, a name with wide rather than limited appeal, or a name that communicates to a large audience rather than a small one.

7. *Choose a name that communicates vibrancy.* Church names that communicate excitement and celebration are attractive to people who are hurting and in need of support. Use a name that includes words like *hope* or *life.* Try using the word *new,* since people like to be part of a pioneering venture. Ask others if your proposed name communicates excitement.

Check with your denominational leaders to see what, if any, regulations they have concerning your name. Take the proper legal steps to file a name change with your state government. Make the necessary change on all the items containing your old name, such as church stationery, bulletins, programs, business cards, brochures, and church signs. Don't continue to use the old stationery until you use it up. If a name change is important, it is important to make the change everywhere as soon as possible.

A First-Impression Piece

The church was ready to close its doors. New guests seldom visited. The morale of the church was too low to encourage significant word-of-mouth exposure of the church's ministry among the unchurched. We didn't have much money, but I determined we would do something to communicate to our community. The answer was a first-impression piece. We designed an introductory brochure about our church and began mailing it to every home in

WHAT'S IN A NAME?

Conduct a survey concerning your name.

1. List the names of all churches in your ministry area.

2. Categorize them based on similarity. For example, all church names with "Grace" in them go in one category, all those with "Community" go in another, and so forth. Some names may appear in more than one category.

3. How many other churches have a name similar to yours? The more there are, the greater likelihood there is confusion about your church's identity in your ministry area.

4. Look at your name from an unchurched person's perspective. What does your name say to him or her? What doesn't it say that you wish it did say?

5. Are there any barriers in your name that might keep people from visiting? A good way to analyze this is to ask some unchurched people what they think about your name.

6. Summarize your findings and determine what needs to be done.

67

our ministry area. At first we had only enough money to mail to about two hundred homes a month. So every month without fail, we systematically mailed it to two hundred different homes in our area. We did this for five years, and it paid off in more guests visiting our church.

A first-impression piece is a great way to say hello to your community. It is a brochure that is given to new people as a way to inform them about your church.

Four out of five readers will look only at the first page of a brochure, so the cover of your first-impression piece must be designed to catch the attention of as many readers as possible so they will read the rest. The cover should include a photo or drawing that illustrates your purpose or mission. Use pictures of people not buildings. Select a title that implies a benefit. For example, "New Hope: The Friendly Church That Cares" implies that there is hope, friendship, and concern at that church. Or "Catch the Spirit of New Life at Community Presbyterian Church," which implies an exciting new approach to life.

Design a church logo that is up-to-date. Ask an art or print professional to review your logo and make suggestions on modernizing it. Consider the design, color, and clarity of its message. Include a statement on the cover that notes some benefits of your church. Why would anyone want to come? What benefits will they receive by attending your church?

The main part of your first-impression piece should give people an overview of your church. Resist the desire to say everything. This is just a "first" impression piece. If it does its job, there will be further opportunities to tell more of your story to the people who begin attending your church. The copy should be readable, in everyday language, with lots of white space around it. Use pictures and titles that are understandable to the primary audience you are targeting. Mention the benefits and special features of your church. A short biography or sketch of your senior pastor and staff photos is always appropriate. If space permits, you may want to include short testimonials from various people in your church, with their pictures if possible.

A statement of your church's purpose or mission written in common language (twenty-five words or less), a simple map showing your church's location, and an overview sketch of your church facilities (essential for larger churches with complex facilities) are good additions. Also consider including:

- brief descriptions of programs and activities for every age group
- photos of your congregation participating in worship and other activities
- stories of how people in your church are being served
- photos and descriptions of your church's service to the community
- a brief schedule of activities
- an invitation to visit
- offers of professional help or services

Design your first-impression piece so that it may be used in a variety of ways. It should be sized so that it fits into a standard business envelope, but include a mailing panel so that it can also be mailed without an envelope. Be sure to include your church's name, complete address, and phone number. Include postal codes and area codes, as well as the times and locations of your programs.

A well-designed first-impression piece is the cornerstone of a church advertising plan. Once it has been designed, plan on mailing it to every home in your ministry area. Mail it out every year in either September or January. If the funds are available, mail the first-impression piece to everyone in your ministry area at the same time. Do this every year without fail, since it takes time to catch the attention of those in your community.

Many churches will find that the money is not available for such a large mailing. In that case they should use the following strategy. The first year mail the first-impression piece to everyone within a five-minute drive of your church building. Then the second year mail it to everyone within a ten-minute drive. Continue on in the third year by sending it to everyone within a fifteen-minute drive. In the fourth year mail it to everyone within a twenty-minute drive. What do you do in the fifth year? Redesign your first-impression piece and start all over again!

The biggest mistake churches make with direct mail is to try it once and forget it. Ultimately what you hope to accomplish is the imprinting of your name and ministry in people's minds, so that when they do want to attend church, they think of your church. Saying hello to your community takes time and patience. Keep mailing first-impression pieces to their homes. It will produce results.

Other forms of advertising can also be good ways to connect with new people.

- *Newspaper ads.* In developing your ads, remember:
  1. Focus on issues unchurched people are concerned with. Do some personal interviews and research on your target audience.

2. Write the ad in the language of the audience you intend to reach. Before you run it, show the copy to unchurched friends to see if it communicates to them and elicits the desired response.

3. Don't place the ad on the church page. Place it in the paper where your target group is most likely to see it.

- *Telemarketing.* In a mass-calling campaign, expect to make ten thousand calls, have one thousand persons express interest, and see fifty to one hundred persons show up to your advertised event.

- *Direct mail.* A well-done direct mail piece will generate a 0.5 to 2.0 percent response. The biggest mistake churches make in using direct mail is not sending out enough pieces. A minimum mailing of ten thousand is needed to receive any measurable response. Mail at least three times a year: early fall, pre-Christmas, and pre-Easter.

- *Internet/website.* Design an attractive website with links to all your programs, ministries, and staff. Use the site to introduce your church to those who may be "surfing" for a church.

Whichever form you use, aim to produce high-quality ads that are simple, creative, and memorable. If necessary, hire a professional agency. See the cost as an investment. All advertising should have a "we-can-help" message.

Connect in Cyberspace

The World Wide Web has become a way of life for millions of people. It is estimated that more than half of all homes in the

United States own at least one PC, with most of them connected to the Internet.

Business entrepreneurs have already cracked the Web, using it to distribute information, communication, products, and services. They see the Internet as a massive opportunity that is only a mouse click away from an extremely large audience. Internet observers are predicting that 20 percent of all household purchases will be made over the Internet by 2007. Some computer consultants say, "If you're not using the Internet today, you won't be in business in ten years."

With the growing number of people using the Internet, wise church leaders will move quickly to establish a ministry in cyberspace. Churches will find the following basic ideas indispensable in the coming years.

Welcome people by email. If you use a registration card or a similar format for guests who visit your church, add a request for the person's email address. Then forget about sending a welcome letter via normal mail and instead send it via email.

Establish a care net. Set up a care network whereby people can communicate needs and receive an appropriate response. Recruit caregivers from your church to answer and respond to email received on your care network. Prayer requests can be passed along to intercessors.

Provide community via chat rooms. Conversations over the Web via chat rooms provide a surprising amount of personal community. Friendships are formed, love is given and received, and people feel accepted through this form of ministry.

Share information. Develop a webpage that people can visit to receive information on your church. Introductory informa-

CREATE A LASTING IMPRESSION

tion should be provided on all ministries and pastoral staff, as well as times of services and directions to your facility. Add regularly updated information on matters of interest to the entire congregation.

Offer educational opportunities. Consider offering classes on your website on Bible study, handling finances, divorce care, family life, and a host of other topics. Not only will such classes serve a sound educational purpose but will also be an introduction to your church.

The Desired Response

Developing a church name that communicates your willingness to serve others and then saying hello through a first-impression piece mailed to everyone in your ministry area as well as through your Internet website are good ways to get started in bringing your church to the attention of the community.

The story is told in advertising circles about a man who found himself in an elevator with Lee Iacocca, then the head of Chrysler. "You're Lee Iacocca, aren't you?" asked the man. The auto executive acknowledged that he was. "Mr. Iacocca," the man spoke up, "I want to tell you how much I enjoy your television commercials." To this compliment, Iacocca replied, "Sir, I could not care less what you think of my commercials. What I want to know is, what kind of car do you drive?"

For Iacocca, if people didn't buy a Chrysler product, the commercials didn't matter. A good church name, an effective first-impression piece, and a creative website are desirable for a church. But if people don't buy the product—life in Christ—it doesn't really matter. Always bear in mind that the important thing is not the advertising but the response.

73

Questions to Ask and Answer

1. What is the purpose of your church?
2. What makes your church unique when compared to other churches in your ministry area?
3. What are some benefits that people could expect to receive from attending your church?
4. What are newer members saying about your church?
5. What do you want the reader to know, think, feel, and do after reading your first-impression piece?
6. What resources do you have available for producing this piece (budget, time, people who can help, equipment, final authority for approvals)?
7. Who will be the primary audience you hope to reach with your advertising piece (families, youth, elderly people, singles, a particular ethnic group, or others)?
8. Has your church started ministry in the cyberculture of the Internet? If not, when are you going to begin? If yes, how can you improve?

6

SPREAD THE WORD

The gospel is still the only key to lasting church growth.

Flavil R. Yeakley, Jr.

Looking for a doctor? Need a home loan? Buying a new car? Selecting a college? Where do you go for advice? Do you look in the paper? Watch TV? Go on the Internet? Or "let your fingers do the walking"? If you are like most people, first you ask a family member, associate, or friend.

Advertisers call this "word of mouth." It is the most effective way of advertising any organization—even a church! Word-of-mouth advertising is referred to in Scripture as a story, a report, a tiding, a reputation, and a rumor. Rumors are characterized as either good or evil (2 Cor. 6:8). Believers are encouraged to think about and spread good rumors (see Phil. 4:8).

Jesus's ministry was communicated predominantly by word of mouth. After Jesus raised a dead man, Luke records: "This report [rumor, story] concerning Him went out all over Judea and in all the surrounding district" (Luke 7:17). Jesus's reputation spread by positive word of mouth, and your church's ministry will too. Every day people talk about your church, its ministries, and its programs. This talk adds to or subtracts from your reputation.

Bad news or good news, people are talking about your church. A classic example of how word-of-mouth advertising affects a church is found in 1 Thessalonians 1:8. Writing about the church in Thessalonica, Paul says, "For the word of the Lord has sounded forth [echoed] from you, not only in Macedonia and Achaia, but also in every place your faith toward God has gone forth." People were telling how the Thessalonians had turned from worshiping idols to serving the living and true God. They were spreading the story by word of mouth. It was so effective that Paul confesses, "We have no need to say anything."

My wife and I were spending a week at a church where I was candidating for the position of pastor. A real-estate salesperson had arranged for us to see several houses in the neighborhood where the church was located. My wife and the real-estate lady were going through one house, and I decided to walk down the block, knock on a few doors, and simply ask people what they knew about the church.

I introduced myself to people as someone who was thinking of purchasing a home in their neighborhood and asked how they liked the area. After a little bit of conversation, I casually asked if they knew anything about the church a few blocks away. Some knew more than others to be sure, but everyone had heard something about the church. One lady said she had heard that the church was going to build a new facility on the vacant land next to it. Others offered insights, such as, "It's rumored to be a nice family church" and "They reportedly keep to themselves."

I had not told anyone that I might become the new pastor, but at one house the lady exclaimed, "Are you the new pastor?" She did not attend the church but knew someone who did and had been told that a new pastor was visiting. Most of the rumors I heard that day were positive ones.

Later I accepted the call to pastor this church, in part due to the reputation it had, which I learned that day by talking to people in the neighborhood.

It's a Small World

A few years ago I was attending a church in Wilmington, North Carolina. Following the worship service, I was introduced to a lady from the church who asked, "I know it's a long shot, but I have a former college roommate who married a pastor and lives in Palm Springs, California. By any chance would you know her?"

When she told me the names of the couple, I realized I knew them. "In fact, I consulted with their church a number of years ago," I said.

The woman exclaimed, "It's a small world, isn't it!"

Yes, it is a small world. I was connected to this woman by one person who lived more than 2,500 miles away. How close are we to other people around the world?

Part of the folklore that has circulated since the 1960s is that we are all connected by just "six degrees," or six people—we are only six people away from knowing anyone in the world. We know someone who knows someone else who in turn knows someone else and so on.

The concept of "six degrees of separation" came from a study conducted by psychologist Stanley Milgram in 1967.

He studied the "small world" phenomenon by asking several hundred people in Boston and Omaha to somehow get a letter to a complete stranger in Boston. They had to send a letter to a personal friend whom they thought would be able to reach the stranger.

Milgram discovered that in most cases, by the time the letter reached the stranger, it had changed hands only six times. He concluded that everyone can be reached by a chain of friends only six links long.

The study was not as conclusive as most people think. Because Milgram's test group was small, there were many unanswered questions. Thus researchers at Columbia University, led by Duncan Watts, conducted a large-scale study using the Internet. The Watts's study asked more than 60,000 people in 163 countries to try to get in touch with one of 18 people located in 13 countries. Of the 24,613 email chains started, only 384 reached their targets. Six reached the target person directly. The success of the other emails ranged from 42 reaching the target person in 2 emails to 3 reaching their destination in 10 emails.

Actually the successful chains required an average of only four steps to get to the targeted person. The researchers concluded that if most of the chains could have been completed, half of them would have reached the target person in five steps, if the sender and the eventual receiver lived in the same country. If the target person lived in a different country, they estimated it would take seven steps.

While the results of the Watts's study are complicated, it appears that Milgram's six degrees of separation conclusion is in the ballpark.

One complication of the study is that of the people who received the unsolicited email, 63 percent did not send it on. Evidently many participants ignored the email, figuring it was spam. With only one-third of the recipients forwarding the email, the chains dwindled quickly with each successive step, until only 2 percent reached their destination.

The research appears to point to the small-world phenomenon as not only real but more universal than anyone would have suspected. Amazingly, for anybody you want to reach in the world, it's likely that someone you know knows someone who knows someone who knows the person.

It cannot be ignored, however, that 98 percent of the emails in the study never reached their destination. Why did the email have such a high failure rate? Of course, the problem may be related to the use of email for the research study. We have all received email chain letters and refused to forward them along to our friends. Yet the issue may go deeper than a frustration with spam and chain letters. When the researchers asked people why they had not forwarded the email, 1 percent indicated they could not think of anyone to send the email to. For many of the rest, it seems likely that the underlying reason the emails floundered is that they just did not want to be bothered.

The study pointed out that, as in most social networks, making the connection is mostly a question of who is willing to help. While it may be true that we can reach about anyone in the world through only six or seven steps, if someone along the way decides not to help out, the chain is broken.

Just because we are only six steps from the Queen of England does not mean we can get a message to her. We can ask our friends for help, such as through an email, but that is all we can do. If someone along the chain decides not to forward our message, it is not going to get there.

The study on six degrees of separation suggests that we are pretty connected. However, the study also points out that we are not really connected. The bottom line is we have numerous people we can build relationships with—if we want to. We have many people we can share the gospel with—if we want to. We have lots of people we can invite to church—if we want to. Unfortunately, most of us just do not want to be bothered.

How Rumors Spread

In our society many of us depend on word of mouth to filter through the many products, ideas, and offers that come our way every day. Studies in the field of diffusion of innovation (how new products spread) have found that people do not choose a product based purely on factual information. The overwhelming majority of people depend on subjective evaluations conveyed to them from other individuals like themselves who have previously adopted a product. It appears that potential adopters rely on the modeling of near-peers who have already adopted a product. New products literally take off after interpersonal networks are activated to spread subjective, positive evaluations.

Churches grow as previous adopters (members and attenders) model their happiness by spreading good rumors (positive word-of-mouth evaluations) to their near-peers who are potential adopters (friends, family, and associates). The spreading talk develops an "echo effect" as word of mouth reverberates back and forth, spilling over to other people who may be interested in your church. Keep the following insights in mind as you consider the impact circulating rumors have on your church and its ministry.

Word of mouth is not based on one thing you do or don't do. It's the result of hundreds of little things you do consistently well. Occasionally short-term rumors may focus on one particular aspect of your ministry. The long-term rumors or word-of-mouth-conversations change slowly, since they depend on the history of ministry found in your church over many years.

You do not have to sit by and wait to hear what people say about you. You can take control by using some of the ideas in this chapter. Word of mouth can be managed. You cannot stop people from talking; thus you must begin to use proactive strategies to manage what people are saying.

Word of mouth does not replace anything you are doing. It supplements and enhances your current efforts in all areas of ministry. Talk alone will never be enough. Reportedly Ralph Waldo Emerson told an acquaintance, "What you are speaks so loud, I can't hear what you say."

The rule of three–thirty-three is always at work. For every three people willing to tell a positive story about an experience with your church, there are thirty-three others who will tell a horror story.[1] For some reason, negative talk reaches a wider audience than positive talk. Of course, the exact numbers may vary from one organization to another.

> For every three people willing to tell a positive story about your church, thirty-three are willing to tell a negative one.

The White House Office of Consumer Affairs finds that a dissatisfied customer reveals the unpleasant experience to nine others. A California market research firm shows that dissatisfied automobile customers tell their stories to twenty-two others. A Dallas researcher says that in banking, a dissatisfied depositor will tell eleven others about a bank mistake and that those eleven tell five more people—an average of fifty-five horror stories.[2]

I'm not aware of any studies that reveal how many other people dissatisfied members of a church tell about their displeasure, but be certain that it does take place. Since human nature tends to change little from one organization to another, it is likely that the figures found by secular organizations are representative of churches also.

People seem conditioned to share the negative aspects of their experience. It takes one hundred positive stories to overcome the impact of one negative one.

Word of mouth travels fast. Researchers think that the average person has a sphere of influence that includes 250 people. This means that if your city has a population of 62,500, by word of mouth you are only two people away from everyone in town. If you tell all 250 people in your sphere of influence and they in turn tell all 250 people in theirs, then everyone in town will know what you talked about (250 x 250 = 62,500). Extending this formula two more steps reveals that each of us is only about 4 or 5 people removed from everyone in the entire world, which is the reason we often say, "It's a small world." When considering how quickly rumors spread by word of mouth, it honestly is small.

Positive word of mouth takes place when you exceed what people expect. Think of a continuum of the service you offer to people (see figure on p. 83). It's not surprising that poor service results in negative rumors. It may shock you to learn that just doing what people expect results in no word of mouth. People won't talk about it since it's what they expected, nothing special. When people receive more service than they expect, they spread good rumors. Excellent service results in positive word of mouth as people express to others their unexpected pleasure at being served well by your church.

Poor Service	Expected Service	Excellent Service
Negative Word of Mouth	No Word of Mouth	Positive Word of Mouth

Some churches have natural word-of-mouth exposure due to their size. In general, a church with a worship attendance above that of the average church in its ministry area will have many positive comments made concerning it. Note the following graph as an example.

There are ten churches depicted in the graph on the next page. The average worship attendance used in the example is 150. For a church to have natural word-of-mouth exposure, it will need to have a worship attendance above 150. It is easy to see that churches B, C, and E are above this 150 mark and will have a natural visibility via word of mouth. Church F is just at the break point of discovering that word of mouth happens quite naturally. The remaining churches will need to work at developing word-of-mouth advertising, since they have too few people for it to develop naturally.

If your church's worship attendance is below the average attendance of all the other churches in your ministry area, then developing positive word-of-mouth talk will be an important factor in the future growth of your church. Also you need to give serious consideration to this aspect of your ministry if current talk about your church is negative or weak. Is your church known in your ministry area? If not, you will need to develop a strategy to help increase your word-of-mouth image.

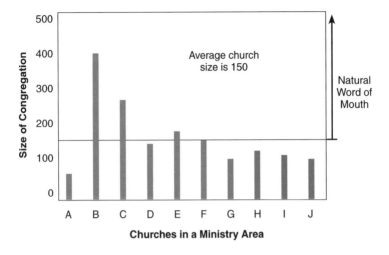

Churches in a Ministry Area

Energizing Good Rumors

ONE LITTLE THING

Launch a "One Little Thing" program for your church. Print a card like the following:

One Little Thing

It often takes just one little thing to make a church more effective. Please answer the following two questions.

One thing I keep hearing others say about our church is . . .

One little thing we could do to address this comment is . . .

Collect the cards and then begin doing the one little thing.

How can a church tie into the network of previous adopters (church members and attenders) to reach potential adopters? As a church leader, you do not need to sit by passively. You can be thoughtful, organized, and systematic about word-of-mouth advertising. Good rumors will develop as present members and attenders sense personal satisfaction with the ministry of your church. Begin by listening to what your members are saying. Energizing good rumors about your church begins inside your church. The word of mouth that is generated by your present members and regular worshipers is a powerful influence on the morale, ministry, and mission of your

84

church. What do your members say about your church to other members? What are they communicating to those outside your church? If you don't know, find out.

Teach your people to avoid negative talk. Negative talk about your church must be avoided no matter how difficult conditions are. When I was a soccer coach, my number one rule was "Never say anything bad about your teammate." The minute teammates start speaking negatively about their team and each other is the moment the team begins to fall apart.

By sacrificially serving each other, we work together to fulfill Christ's command to make disciples of all the nations. Negative talk about each other and our church, even if done with innocent motives, causes serious damage. Once our members start bad-mouthing our church, nonmembers pick it up and pass it along with more fury, since they heard it right from the source. Make it clear to people what the Bible says about negative talk (James 3:1–12) and how it affects the growth of your church. Train them to say the right things. Explain the proper way to bring disagreements to the church leadership. Don't bad-mouth other churches from your pulpit. Preach the positive side of things more than the negative. You don't need to be blind to or totally ignore the negatives but always create an atmosphere that stresses the positive, more productive side.

Share good news about your church as it happens. A newsletter is a solid way to build a cadre of loyal followers. It is time consuming but is certainly worth the effort. One key is regularity. Many churches put out a newsletter sporadically. If anything, this works against the development of good rumors.

In a newsletter make good use of pictures. Keep it crisp, clean, clear, and upbeat. Feature stories that share good news about what is happening in your ministry. Be especially alert to stories about people who illustrate your loving care and service to each other.

Interviewing people from the platform on Sunday mornings is another way to share good stories about your church. Select new people, those with a fresh testimony and those who have been served effectively by your church. Host an end-of-the-year event when many people who have been touched by your church share their stories. As members hear these real stories, they will naturally share them by word of mouth to others, thus passing on the good news about your church's ministry.

Reach out in ministry to community leaders. One pastor visited the mayor of his city. After the proper introductions were made, the mayor asked how he could help the pastor. The pastor confided that he simply wanted to know how the mayor was doing. Before leaving, he prayed for the mayor. The mayor was shocked and pleased. Needless to say, this opinion leader has good things to say about this pastor and his church.

Host a thank-you dinner for community leaders, such as firemen, policemen, and city council members—not as a time to register complaints but for thanking them for a job well done in serving the people of your city or community.

Build good experiences and memories for your people. The DWYPYWD principle builds trust and promotes positive word of mouth. It means, Do what you promised you would do. Complete projects that are started. Work on small goals that are sure to succeed and publicize their fulfillment. Take pictures of church events. Show them at meetings throughout the year. Develop a video about your church.

Host open houses where members share their desires, hopes, and concerns. At the same meetings, church leaders can communicate their church's vision and direction, thereby starting good rumors that will be shared again and again.

Remove any negative signs from your church property and literature. Look around your church and see how many times you count the word *no.* Do you have "No Smoking" or "No Parking" signs? If you have signs that give a negative message hanging on your walls or posted on your property, take them down. If they are printed in your bulletin, program, or newsletter, take them out. It is difficult to build positive word of mouth about your church if negative messages are hanging on the walls.

Communicate victories no matter how small or seemingly insignificant. Print answers to prayer. Share how your church is progressing toward its yearly goals. Tell how ministries are reaching people. Publicly read thank-you cards and letters from people who have been helped by your church. Develop a sense of expectancy by preaching messages that point to hope in the Lord. Describe how God has met church needs over the years and project his certain help into the future. Tell how God has answered your prayers.

Provide business cards for every member of the church as a tool for developing good rumors. Give each person in your church, including children, fifty-two cards. Everyone is important enough for this tiny investment. People feel important when they have a card, and they'll use it to spread the good word about your church. Encourage people to hand out one card each week with an invitation to attend your worship services. Not only will they hand them to family and friends, but the cards will start showing up in other places too. People will give them to their postman, gas station attendant, and dentist. The first time you find a guest who came as a result of the business card, be sure to make it well known.

Exceed expectations. Wal-Mart has capitalized on this by hiring older people to stand at the doors to greet people as they come in. These grandfatherly and grandmotherly people make a special fuss over children and offer you a friendly greeting along with a shopping cart. At the beginning this service went beyond what anyone expected. Now other stores are offering the same service.

Why not hand out a rose to each lady who attends your church, not just on Mother's Day but on other Sundays too? Prepare a special coloring book for children. Don't go out and buy one, have one designed with a story about your church and your children's ministry. Then give each child who worships with you a small box of crayons and your coloring book as a special gift. Take a video of the children doing something special during Sunday school, then show it after church on several televisions near your refreshment table. Give copies to all parents who want one.

For certain, we know that people tell others—lots of others—about their experience at your church. The only action you can take to create positive word of mouth is to offer a ministry that makes every person take notice. This happens only when a church plans on taking people beyond the first visit.

Questions to Ask and Answer

1. How can your church energize good rumors? Choose ideas from this chapter or come up with others and begin implementing them.

2. Spend some time looking over your church's literature and signs posted on walls and church grounds. Look for

any that say, No! Do you have signs with the actual word *no* in them? If so, make a list of them. Look for:

No smoking
No skateboarding
No parking
No dancing
No food or beverages
No running
No talking

3. Are there other ways you may be saying no to people?
4. What variations of these and other signs are found around your church? What is the message they are relating to people? Are there ways to say the same message in a positive manner?

7

Start New Ministries

The scope of who it is that God means to invite to the feast,
you see, is not ours to define. We are not put in charge of the
guest list.

Don C. Skinner

Just 130 years ago (March 7, 1876), the telephone was considered the most valuable patent ever issued. It's hard to believe,
but back in 1879 there were no telephone numbers. The first telephone operators had to memorize the names of all subscribers. A
measles epidemic changed all that when a doctor recommended
assigning numbers to the townspeople in case the operator got
ill. Today the telephone is so much a part of our lives that it is
almost unthinkable to do without one.

In 1955 many churches began using the telephone for ministry by broadcasting recorded prayers continuously over the
telephone. By the early sixties, churches across the United States
were offering "dial-a-prayer" services.

Telecare

The telephone is a super example of how churches have developed new ways of effectively serving people — Christians and non-Christians. Telemarketing has been used to plant new churches, reach out to the unchurched, and care for church members. With home visitation declining due to increased neighborhood crime, commuting, and the saturation of contacts experienced in everyday life, there is a resistance to anyone stopping by for an unannounced visit. As a result many churches use the telephone as a means of pastoral care for their members. It has been discovered that phone calls have about the same appeal as a personal visit. A phone call offers the contact, the encouragement, and the image of a visit, while respecting people's personal space. Churches are using personal phone calls to follow up on guests and perform basic pastoral care. It is another form of care that transcends pastoral and lay visitation.

"Telecare" is the name given to pastoral care completed by phone. You might consider using this means of providing basic care for your people. Here are a few steps to implementation:

1. Identify callers and select key leadership personnel to oversee the program. Choose people for the ministry who like to talk on the phone. Recruit people by phone to hear how they sound. Don't overlook shut-ins as possible callers.
2. Train callers in a few sessions of about two hours each. Teach people to understand the power of words, listening skills, and how to keep a record of their calls. Practice by having callers phone each other, using phones in different offices at church or cell phones. Provide a basic outline of questions to ask or ideas to talk about.

3. Callers can use their own phones or church phones. In some cases it may be helpful to install an extra line at church dedicated to pastoral care.

4. Contact active and inactive members, shut-ins, teenagers, excited people, apathetic people, quiet ones, and compulsive talkers. As people in society in general continue to withdraw, the church is going to play a vital role in overcoming the loneliness that will result. The telephone may be an instrument your church can use to reach people in your community.

> In most cases it will take new ministries to reach new people for Christ.

THINK ABOUT IT

Eight Questions

Telecare is just one example of a ministry form being used to serve others with the love of Christ. There are countless ways to serve people. A long time ago Christ called his disciples' attention to the readiness of others to learn about the gospel. Watching a group of people walking toward them, he said, "The harvest is plentiful, but the workers are few. Therefore beseech the Lord of the harvest to send out workers into His harvest" (Matt. 9:37–38).

The harvest is ready. People are open and eager to respond. We just need to open our eyes and begin looking for them. In most cases it takes the starting of new ministries to attract new people and give them an opportunity for the love of Christ to be shown. But what ministry should you start? Here are eight questions to answer.

Question One

Who is our audience? Reaching the whole world with the gospel is the mission of the Christian faith, but life-giving churches recognize that the world is made up of many different audiences. Since different groups of people have quite different cultures, needs, and methods of communication, a church that intentionally tries to reach a specific group with the message of Christ will normally be much more effective than one that tries to reach everyone with a general outreach. Every church should have a sign that says, "Everyone Welcome," but unless they have a deliberate strategy in place to help people become a part of the church, they will see only accidental growth.

At first glance, it may seem that aiming at select groups of people is not biblical. On further reflection, however, it becomes obvious that it is the only strategic way to actually reach the world for Christ. Think for a moment of how God began to redeem the world. From the beginning, God has been concerned for the entire world, not just for certain people. God's desire is to redeem every tribe, nation, people, and family on the face of the earth. Yet how did he go about reaching the world? His plan started with a clearly defined target audience in the person and family of Abram and worked outward to the whole world from there. Abram became a family, then a tribe, and eventually a nation among all the nations of the world. God said, "I will also make You a light of the nations so that My salvation may reach to the end of the earth" (Isa. 49:6).

The coming of Jesus through the nation of Israel was the key to bringing blessing to all the nations of the world. Indisputably, "God so loved the world, that He gave His only begotten Son, that whoever believes in Him shall not perish, but have eternal life" (John 3:16). Jesus loved the entire world not just certain select segments of it. He eventually would die for "our sins; and not for ours only, but also for those of the whole world" (1 John 2:2).

To reach the whole world, Jesus began with a defined target audience. His niche was among the Israelites, specifically Galileans, his clearly defined target audience. It's interesting that Jesus selected twelve men who displayed both a heterogeneous and a homogeneous mix. Matthew was an establishment type, Simon the Zealot had a revolutionary background, John may have come from aristocratic stock, and Peter, James, and John were all blue-collar workers. Yet they were all Galileans. No Gentile, Samaritan, Idumean, or even a Hellenistic Jew was part of the Twelve. Jesus gathered an inner circle of men who were a clearly definable target—Galileans. They all spoke Aramaic (Matt. 26:73; Mark 14:70; Luke 22:59). The only exception in the Twelve was Judas Iscariot (he was not Galilean but came from Kerioth, somewhere south of Judea). Later the chosen replacement for Judas was a Galilean named Matthias (Acts 1:23–26). Similar to how God chose Abraham and his family, Jesus used a clear target audience to begin winning the world.

Paul's blueprint for ministry involved targeting a specific group of people to reach the whole world. His heart's desire was always to see the Jews come to faith in Christ (see Rom. 10:1). To him, the gospel was for everyone in the world but needed to go to the Jews first, as he declared, "For I am not ashamed of the gospel, for it is the power of God for salvation to everyone who believes, to the Jew first and also to the Greek" (1:16). Paul's unique calling, however, was to the Greeks or Gentiles. Christ told Ananias that Paul was to be "a chosen instrument of Mine, to bear My name before the Gentiles and kings and the sons of Israel" (Acts 9:15).

Paul wove his love for the Jews and his calling to the Gentiles into an original strategy. His usual custom was to go first to a synagogue to preach and then move from there to the Gentile

God-fearers (Acts 9:20; 13:5; 14:1; see especially 17:1–3). To reach the Gentiles, Paul targeted the Jewish synagogue community where he knew there would be God-fearing Gentiles and Gentile proselytes to Judaism. The Jews rejected Paul (except for a few people) in most situations, but he would win considerable numbers of the Gentiles and form them into a new church. Paul effectively used a plan that targeted Gentiles involved to some degree in the synagogue communities to which he spoke.

While Paul seemed to reach out naturally to a specific group of people, most churches must think strategically through questions like: Who is our church's primary target audience(s)? In what ways is our church reaching members of our target audience for Christ? How might our church be more faithful in communicating the gospel to our audience(s)? Having an understanding of one's target audience is a way of determining the most effective methods of winning people to Christ, while remaining open to supernatural encounter and prayer. Remember the proverb: "The mind of man plans his way, but the LORD directs his steps" (Prov. 16:9). A strategic plan is important, but authentic church growth is always supernaturally empowered.

Of course, a church should not be tied so rigidly to a plan or target group that it is insensitive when the life-giving Spirit leads in other directions. While it is biblical to have a clear target audience, it is evident that the Holy Spirit also directs in supernatural ways.

Question Two

Where do we sense the burden of God in our church at this time? The number one attitude seen in a church that does a good job welcoming newcomers is the desire to reach out to others. Caring service is the center of all that they do. A church desiring to serve others should seek God's leading and wisdom and carefully evaluate resources and abilities to implement a new ministry.

God desires to use our gifts and abilities to serve others. Carl George, respected church consultant, once noted that in Luke 10:25–37, Jesus tells us not to ask, "Whom am I required to love?" ("Who is my neighbor?"), but "How can I show the love of Christ to others?" ("To whom am I a neighbor?").

Question Three

What specific group of people is God giving us a burden to serve? Different people have different needs. Gone are the days of thinking broadly. It is now time to think specifically. At one time churches developed a one-size-fits-all ministry for adults. Later we thought in terms of a ministry for younger adults, middle-aged adults, and senior adults. Now we must view adult ministry even more specifically. Young adults can be divided into several categories, such as collegians, career singles, young couples without children, young couples with children, and single parents.

Middle-aged adults are never-married singles, couples with elementary-school children, couples with junior highers, couples with senior highers, couples with college-age children, empty-nest couples, and single parents.

Older adults include the recently retired, adults living in care facilities, adults living with their children, adults raising their grandchildren, and on and on. A church cannot say it wants to minister to adults. Today you must be very specific about the type of adult to whom you want to minister.

Of course churches like to think of ministering to all people, and in a sense they do. Yet studies of healthy churches indicate that there must be a clear focus of ministry identity.[1] While that target can be expanded some, there must be a limited number of ministry focus points, or a church will lose its magnetism. Thus, even in churches that say they minister to everyone, it is easy to identify their primary focus.

Question Four

What needs do these people have that we could meet? If you don't know what the needs are, ask the people. Sticking to your own idea of what people want without asking them for their input is a mistake. Not all new ministries end up in the Hall of Fame. Some end up in the Hall of Shame.

A number of years ago, one church attempted to begin a coffeehouse for local college students as a means of serving them and sharing the good news of Jesus Christ. It was called The Out House Coffee House. Church leaders just assumed the college students wanted a coffeehouse and moved quickly forward with plans, never thinking to survey them to discover their needs. As you might guess, the coffeehouse ministry was a disaster. Even though the publicity, invitations, food, music, and people were all in place, no one came to the coffeehouse. It was not what the collegians needed or wanted. If church leaders had asked them earlier, it would have saved a great deal of time, effort, and money, not to mention the embarrassment suffered from a failed attempt at starting a new ministry.

As you do research in your community to determine your target audiences and their needs, a helpful process is to complete a chart like the following.

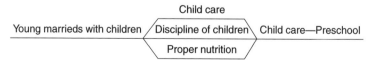

Young marrieds with children | Child care / Discipline of children / Proper nutrition | Child care—Preschool

On the left write the audience you want to reach through a new ministry. In the example above, the church wants to begin a new ministry for young married couples with children. After interviewing young married couples to determine their needs, the church listed three needs that the target audience has. They discovered that young couples with children needed help with day care, understanding how to discipline children, and learning how to prepare nutritional meals.

Once the needs have been determined, the next step is to look at your church's resources. Do you have the people, finances, knowledge, skills, and facilities to meet any of the three needs listed? As you research the available resources, God will direct you toward the needs you can properly address. Write on the right side of the chart the ministry your church will pursue. As you can see in the illustration above, the church decided they had the resources to meet the need of day care by providing a preschool for their target audience.

Several of these charts could be developed for different groups of people, which would allow your church to see what resources are available. I have found that most churches can start only one new ministry a year. Some larger churches may be able to begin two or three new ministries, but that would be rare. In some situations an older ministry can simply be retooled to meet the needs of a new audience, and in such cases more than one new ministry may get started.

Question Five

What specific ministry are we qualified to start that fits with God's burden and the people we wish to serve? People in a church like to think that they can care for everyone. In a general way churches do care for people from the cradle to the grave. But when it comes to beginning a new ministry, we must think strategically. The fields are truly ripe for harvest. People are hurting and need to be loved and served in ways that will draw them to the Great Shepherd—Jesus Christ. No church has all the necessary resources—money, people, time, knowledge, skill—to do everything that can be proposed. Thus we need to investigate as many ministry opportunities as reasonable before deciding which one to pursue. Talk with leaders from other churches who are already doing the ministry and, if possible, even participate in their ministry for a short time. While you are doing your research, prayerfully ask God what he wants your church to do.

The following list, offered by Carl George, has some potential ministry areas you could consider. Look them over, asking God to burden you with the ones that your church should pursue.

Ministry Areas to Consider

___Prison ministry	___Illiterate
___Homeless	___Other "people groups"
___Abused children	___Athletes
___Unemployed	___Executives
___Abused spouses	___International executives
___English as a second language	___Politicians
___Substance abuse: alcohol, eating disorders, drugs, tobacco	___Artists
	___Homemakers
___International students	___Broadcast and print media
___Terminally ill	___Students
___Homosexuals	___University faculty
___Single parents	___Refugees
___Unwed mothers	___Premarital counseling
___Financial counseling	___Separated and divorced people
___Prenatal/postnatal	___Handicapped

___Crisis pregnancy   ___Hospital visitation

___Medical care   ___Widows/widowers

___Mothers of preschoolers   ___Orphans

___Elderly   ___Incest victims

___Women who have had abortions   ___Hungry people

___AIDS victims   ___Crisis counseling

___Trauma victims

Question Six

What similar ministries are other churches or individuals already doing? A young seminary student and his wife approached me for advice in planting a new church. During our conversation I learned that she was going to head up the children's ministry. I suggested several churches with well-run children's ministries for her to visit. Later, after she had done as I suggested, she shared with me her excitement in seeing how others were doing this ministry. It changed her entire outlook and stretched her vision of what she wanted to organize in the new church.

I still remember her telling me about a church that used a Sesame Street approach to children's ministry. The church had invested a great deal of money in remodeling a large education room into a soundstage where actors, similar to those on Sesame Street, acted out Bible lessons, teaching children in a format that held their attention. By visiting this church, the young wife had an entirely new idea of how to do a children's ministry.

Once God gives you an idea of a ministry you could start, investigate other churches doing similar ministries. Talk with those involved. Learn what is working and not working. What types of responses, roadblocks, and problems might you expect. Learn all you can from these ministries.

Question Seven

What will be our strategy and plan? Study your target group and put together a plan to reach them, beginning with a specific need. Everything doesn't need to be planned before you get started serving others, but do consider the resources of your people, their time, commitment, knowledge, skills, and money. Do not allow your desire to know everything beforehand to squelch the burden and momentum for ministry that has been growing. Learn by doing.

Question Eight

What process do we need to follow to get approval from our church? Understand and follow the process for ministry approval from your church. Go ahead and start your ministry so that leaders will know you are serious and know what you are doing. Leaders will want to give you suggestions, advice, and ideas. Some may even wish to get involved. After approval, be certain to keep leaders informed on the progress of the ministry.

The AAAA Plan

A simple strategy to use in planning a new ministry is the AAAA plan. (See a diagram of the AAAA plan on the next page.)

Advertise

Begin by advertising your new ministry where the people you are trying to serve will be found. As an example, let's assume your church wants to reach young single mothers. After discovering that they are concerned with keeping their children off drugs,

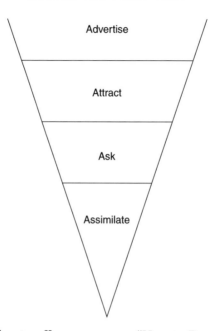

you might plan to offer a course on "How to Drug Proof Your Child." To attract them, you must advertise where single mothers will be found. Announcements on your church bulletin board or a flier in your church program will not likely find the audience you hope to reach. Instead, place your advertising in laundromats and day-care centers. Distribute fliers at park playgrounds, in apartment complexes, and in grocery stores.

Underpromise in your advertising and overdeliver in your ministry. Nothing is more important to people than your keeping your promise. People want churches to do what they say they are going to do. Nothing makes people sadder than when a church doesn't follow through on what it promised to do. Keeping your word is worth more than all the smiles and donuts in the world. Advertising will bring people to you one time, but you must have the goods (the product) when they arrive, or they will not be back.

LOOKING AT THE HARVEST

God has placed your church in a particular location among particular groups of people who are ripe for the harvest. Open your eyes and begin to see the harvest around you by doing the following:

1. Take your church leaders on a windshield tour of your community. Drive slowly through the community and make a list of the various people and potential needs you see.
2. Spend a week reading your local newspaper, jotting down all the different groups of people and specific needs that are reported in news stories.
3. Make an appointment with your local fire chief, police chief, and mayor. When you meet with them, tell them your church is ready and willing to serve others in your community. Ask for ideas on how you can serve others.
4. Randomly call two hundred homes in your community, introduce yourself, and tell people your church wants to serve its community. Ask for ideas on needs and ways your church could be helpful to others.
5. Survey your church members, asking them to note the concerns and needs of people they know.

Summarize your findings. What groups of people did you find? What are their needs? Which needs does it appear your church could begin to serve? Where has God directed your hearts?

Attract

Attracting the people you want to serve happens initially when you offer an event that speaks to a felt need in their lives. Young single mothers in large cities often fear the prospect of their children obtaining and using drugs, sometimes even in elementary school. While their ultimate need is for salvation in Christ, they may not be attracted to a church offering them a Bible study in Genesis, even with free child care. Designing a course or event that speaks directly to a felt need in their lives has a greater ability to attract them.

103

This type of event should have an atmosphere that is non-churchy, informal, and nonthreatening. Prayers and religious-sounding language, if used at all, should be used sparingly. Casual dress appropriate to the people you are serving and a location that is on their turf are best. New people are attracted to events that don't take up their entire day and don't ask for long-term commitments. Short seminar or workshop presentations are most attractive.

Ask

To faithfully serve new people, you must move past advertisement and attraction and ask them to become involved in your new ministry. A three-hour seminar on how to drug proof your child is only the start. The new ministry takes shape when you develop relationships with the new people. While some good tips can be learned in a three-hour seminar, everyone knows that keeping children off drugs is a long-term project. By asking (inviting) those who participate in your attraction event to become involved in a small support group or other ministry, you begin the process of building a relationship that will lead many to Christ.

Assimilate

Assimilating the new people into the life of your church takes place naturally when new people are able to develop friends in your church, join a group or class, and become involved in serving others. By asking people to become involved in a support group, you accomplish two of these three things. They develop friends and have a group with which they identify. As you encourage them to find their own place of service in your group, they will be assimilated into the life of your church.[2]

Questions to Ask and Answer

1. What target group are you going to serve?
2. How do you plan to reach them?
3. What preparation have you done?
4. What resources do you need?
5. Who will serve with you?
6. When do you plan to start?

8

GUESTERIZE YOUR CHURCH

I have finally learned to accept people as they are. Whatever they are in the world, a prostitute, a prime minister, it is all the same to me. But sometimes I see a stranger coming up the road, and I say, "Oh, Jesus Christ, is it you again?"

Russian Monk

When I conduct a church-growth consultation with a local church, I like to visit the church unannounced on a Sunday morning. This gives me the opportunity to feel the atmosphere of the worship service, observe the way newcomers are greeted, walk through the buildings, monitor traffic flow, and observe the church with guest eyes.

A few years ago I visited a church with a worship attendance of 930. The large, prominent buildings caught my attention as I drove into the parking lot. After finding a parking space to my liking—close to a church entrance—I walked toward the building, encountering many other people exiting their cars and heading into church. Since I had never been to this church before, I did not know exactly where to enter the building, so I followed the general flow of traffic. Making my way into the patio area, I wandered through and around groups of people conversing eagerly with each other. Eventually I walked outside and around the perimeter of the church property. All the way I encountered people coming and going to classes, the parking lot, and the sanctuary. Never once did anyone stop to talk to me. Some smiled as our eyes met, but not a single word was spoken. As I approached the back entrance, I spotted the pastor standing outside with a Styrofoam cup of coffee in his hand greeting people excitedly. When we were close enough, he reached out his hand and whispered, "I hope I'm not the first one to greet you today." He was!

How to Guesterize

Being nice to people is just the beginning of connecting people to your church. The people I encountered were all nice people. They smiled at me. I had no reason to assume they were unkind. But being nice and smiling accounts for only about 20 percent, at most, of actually connecting guests to a church. The important thing is to design systems that provide excellent service to those who attend your church. And nowhere is this more important than when you welcome newcomers on their first visit. Systematic approaches to serving others are 80 percent of the battle. We must guesterize our church.

> Guest•er•ize ('gest-er-ize), *vt*: to make a church more responsive to its guests and better able to attract new ones. *syn* see service, care, love, acceptance.

Guesterizing your church occurs when you make guests the most important people at your church on Sunday morning. It means responding to their needs in a manner that causes them to enjoy their time with you. It means giving superior service so that they want to move beyond the first visit. To guesterize your church, I recommend that you give your guests the following.

The Best Attitude

Give your guests the best attitude. They will notice immediately the prevailing attitude—the tone they sense as they walk up to the church building, are greeted on entering the front door, sit in the sanctuary, and meet others. As mentioned previously, most guests will make a judgment about your church within thirty seconds of entering the front door. Their judgment is not made on any scientific evidence slowly gathered over weeks, months, or even years. Their judgment is made quickly based on the attitude or atmosphere they experience. It is made subliminally in the first few moments they experience your church.

One of the major needs people have is to know there is hope for tomorrow. They come to your church looking for encouragement. They want practical advice on how to make it through the week. They want to know that God has not given up on them. Do your preaching, music, friendliness, and people reflect an attitude of hope? Of course, the Bible is a book of hope. Its main message is that God loves us and has a plan for our lives. It tells us that no matter how desperate our lives, God is in the picture, making it turn out right (see Rom. 8:28).

Atmosphere is also created by the facility. Stained glass windows and dark wooden doors do not make for an initial open, friendly feeling. Clear glass doors and windows allow those walking up to or driving by the building to see inside, making the building seem more accessible. Small lobbies (foyers) seem cramped, often making a new person feel too exposed and under pressure. If you want to guesterize your church, I suggest you work on developing an atmosphere of hope and care, as well as opening up your facility to make it feel warm and friendly.

> Being nice and friendly accounts for only about 20 percent of a church's effectiveness in welcoming guests. The other 80 percent comes from well-designed systems.

The Best Communication

As a church consultant, I visit several churches every year. One of my favorite techniques is to station myself in a busy part of the auditorium or foyer to see how many people will speak to me. In many cases, people will walk toward me, our eyes meet, and then they will look toward the ground and walk on by. At other times they will smile as they go by. If this is happening in your church, it has the effect of making your guests feel like nonpersons. They will not perceive you as a friendly church.

If you want to guesterize your church, I suggest that you follow the "Ten-Foot Rule" and the "Just Say Hi" policy. Teach your people, whenever they come within ten feet of a person they do not know, to just say hi. While this will not totally guesterize your church, at least it will let newcomers know they are noticed.

The Best Welcome

I was very tired. As I sat down in the auditorium, my only desire was to be left alone to worship. To my horror the pastor asked all guests to stand. Then one by one he went around the room asking each of us to introduce ourselves and to give a short word of greeting to the congregation. Even though I am a seasoned churchgoer, it was more than embarrassing. I wondered how others felt.

In today's society it is good to welcome guests from the pulpit but not to have them stand to be recognized. Give guests freedom to relax and enjoy the worship service. Whatever you do, take great pains not to embarrass the newcomer. Among other things this means you should not identify new people by placing a ribbon, flower, or nametag on them. Do not ask visitors to stand and speak before the entire congregation. A survey of one thousand adults eighteen years of age or older reported that "making a speech" was the number one event causing adults to be nervous. It ranked first, ahead of, in order, getting married, interviewing for a job, going to the dentist, a first date, and getting a divorce.[1] If you want to guesterize your church, welcome your guests, but do not embarrass them in any way.

The Best Parking

In our age of the automobile, three things continue to be true about most people. First, people do not like to walk more than one block to church. Second, people will drive around for several minutes to find a parking place close to the entrance. Third, if they do not find a parking space where they want it, they will drive on by without stopping. If you want to guesterize your church, I suggest you reserve approximately 5 percent of your parking places for guests as close to your main entrance as possible. And clearly mark them for first- or second-time guests.

The Best Seats

The most popular seats on an airplane are the aisle seats, because people want to feel free to move; we don't like feeling trapped. It is related to our need for personal space—the space around our bodies. Most of the time we guard this space, allowing only privileged others to enter it. This is why we feel more comfortable hugging a family member than an individual we do not know well. Newcomers worshiping in our churches like to protect their personal space as well. When we force them to sit close to another person or in the middle seats, we invade their personal space and make them feel very uncomfortable. Unfortunately, they attribute their discomfort to our church and are not likely to return.

Guests prefer the aisle seats and the seats in the rear of the auditorium because these seats allow them to protect their personal space. However, that is the exact place most regular attenders like to sit! If you want to guesterize your church, I suggest you reserve the aisle seats and the rear seats for guests. Encourage your regular attenders to sit in the middle of longer rows, and leave the best seats for guests.

The Best Time

At the end of one church service, the pastor gave the closing benediction and then said to the audience: "Remember the Five-Minute Rule." This intrigued me since I had never heard of a Five-Minute Rule. I later found out that the people of the church had been instructed to speak to guests during the first five minutes following each worship service. They were not to do any church business or talk to their friends until five minutes

had elapsed. If you want to be a church that sees guests return-
ing, I suggest you reserve the first five minutes following every
worship service for interacting with them.

The Best Service

Recently I visited a rather large church in Southern California. As my wife and I stepped up on the curb to enter the
front door, a lady greeted us by saying, "Hi! Is this your first
time with us?" After we answered yes, she introduced herself,
asked our names, and walked with us into the building to a
welcome center.

At the welcome center she introduced us by name to the
person at the desk, who immediately offered help and gave us
directions to important areas of the church, such as the restrooms
and the auditorium.

As we were about to finish our conversation at the welcome
center, an usher walked up, and the person behind the desk
introduced us by name to him. He then led us to our seats in
the auditorium.

In just a few minutes we had been introduced to several very
friendly people, had our names mentioned three times, and were
given all the initial information we needed.

While you may not follow exactly this church's procedure,
if you want to guesterize your church, I suggest you follow the
three principles they used:

- Approach new people promptly.
- Offer help and information.
- Introduce them by name to others.

Typically, when churches serve their guests well, they provide the following:

Parking attendants. These workers do more than help guests find a good parking place. Most important, they must be ready to welcome guests the moment they step out of their cars with a warm smile and good directions into the building.

Greeters. Selected for their outgoing and friendly personality, these people should meet guests just outside the church building in warm weather and just inside the building in cold weather. Their prime role is to break the ice with newer guests and walk with them into the church building to the welcome table. Drop the word *greeters*; begin to use the word *hosts*. The implication of the term will help those who welcome guests to realize that their responsibility does not begin and end with a smile and a handshake.

Concierge desk. Everyone who has traveled widely is used to a concierge desk in hotels, where they can find assistance in obtaining tickets to attractions, directions to museums, information on places to dine, and countless helpful suggestions. So why not use the same idea in a church by developing a similar point of contact where guests can find assistance in connecting with small groups, ministry teams, and service opportunities? A concierge desk is more than an information table or welcome booth in the sense that specific help is given to directly connect the guest with the services or ministries of the church.

Welcome table. The people who host a welcome table should express appreciation to new people. These hosts must know the answers to everything a new person might ask. The most frequently asked questions include: Where are the restrooms? Where is the sanctuary? Where do the children go? Information about your church and all ministries should be available at this table in brochure form.

Ushers. Ushers are responsible for the comfort and care of guests once they enter the worship area. Above all, they should be friendly and not shy. They should give people a program and any information a new person may need to know about the worship service.

Pulpit welcome. Often first-time guests feel uneasy attending a church's worship service. The role of the pastor or person giving a welcome from the pulpit is mainly to put the new person at ease. Guests should be welcomed and encouraged to relax and enjoy the worship service. Be sure to tell guests that the offering is for members only. Advise new people of any information or irregularities about worship in your church. Remember: do not embarrass them.

Refreshment table. Most guests are quick to leave the sanctuary and church building following the worship service. To encourage them to stay longer, offer a refreshment table with coffee, juice, and snacks. When people have a cup of coffee in one hand and a donut in the other, they will typically stay around until they finish their refreshment. It is best if the refreshment table is located immediately outside the sanctuary or in the back where guests must pass by it on their way out of the church.

Introducers. These people are outgoing, friendly, and warm people, just like the hosts and ushers. Their responsibility is to introduce new guests they meet to at least one other person in your church. While this can take place anywhere in the church, they should position themselves around the refreshment table, as it offers opportunities to meet and talk in a relaxed atmosphere.

Guest luncheon. If fellowship is a high value at your church, and you have a strong family-like corporate culture, consider offering a guest luncheon for first-, second-, and third-time attendees. Tickets (free of course) might be distributed to all guests as they are welcomed. An announcement from the pulpit or in the program could be made that free tickets are available at the concierge desk, welcome table, or information booth. Regular worshipers who bring a friend to church should also be invited to attend the luncheon with their guest. Use a creative name like R U New Cafe to attract attention and interest.

Celebration balloons. It is common to see strings of helium-filled balloons attracting your attention to RV sales and used car lots around town. Does your church have something to celebrate? Why not get folks into the mood with columns of colorful balloons reaching heavenward? How about a great arch of balloons leading into the building? "We had to celebrate and rejoice, for this brother of yours was dead and has begun to live, and was lost and has been found" (Luke 15:32). It is celebration time![2]

Piped-out music. "Install a number of strategically placed outdoor speakers that can welcome people to God's house with the music of heaven. If your church has a recording of your own worship band or musical group, use it. Otherwise, there is a lot of great Christian music available."[3]

Guest information packet. "Every church should have an attractive packet prepared specifically for newcomers. The basic questions your guests are asking should be answered in

CHECK IT OUT

Put a checkmark in the appropriate column below.

	We have	We don't have
Parking attendants	☐	☐
Hosts	☐	☐
Concierge desk	☐	☐
Welcome table	☐	☐
Welcome table host	☐	☐
Ushers	☐	☐
Pulpit welcome	☐	☐
Refreshment table	☐	☐
Introducers	☐	☐
Guest luncheon	☐	☐
Celebration balloons	☐	☐
Piped-out music	☐	☐
Guest information packet	☐	☐
Church tour	☐	☐

this kit: What kinds of things are going on in this church? (The more the better.) Is there a place for my kids? (If not, nothing else matters.) How can I learn more about this church? (See "church tour" below.) One of the best ways to answer all these questions is with a video brochure—a well-produced 8 to 10 minute introduction to the church with words from the pastor, staff, and some new members."[4]

Church tour. "Newcomers are hesitant to wander around a new church uninvited, even though they would like to. So why not offer a short tour of the facilities after each service? Such a tour is a low-commitment, limited-time, high-information event for anyone interested in learning more about your church.

The tour leader guides the group through various halls and rooms, explaining what activities take place there throughout the week. During the tour, it's natural for guests to ask questions about various ministries or upcoming events."[5]

Everyone a Greeter

Everyone in your church should be a greeter. Or a better way to put it is that everyone in your church should be willing to serve others. A pastor told me how he accomplished this in his church. He began by mailing a letter to one-fourth of his regular worshipers asking them to pay special attention to new guests attending their church on the first Sunday of the month. The next week he mailed a similar letter to another fourth of his congregation asking them to welcome guests on the second Sunday of the month. He did this for another fourth of the congregation on the third Sunday and another fourth on the fourth Sunday. In the following months he mailed a postcard to the same people with a friendly reminder that the next Sunday was their Sunday to greet guests. This took

---

HOW TO GET GOOD AT GUESTERIZING

1. Rehearse the principles of guesterizing (found in this chapter in the section How to Guesterize), until you have them memorized.
2. Teach the principles to your leaders, asking them to evaluate your church's success at fulfilling each one.
3. Each month review one principle.
4. Teach your worshipers the Five-Minute Rule and use it.
5. Teach your worshipers the Ten-Foot Rule and the Just Say Hi policy and use them.
6. Assemble a task force of people who have been in your church less than one year and ask them to design a new system for welcoming guests.

place for an entire year. Several months into this process, a lady approached the pastor commenting, "Pastor, it wasn't even my Sunday to greet people and I found myself doing it." This happened with many people. It created an interest in and awareness of welcoming guests to church.

In addition to greeting others, every member of your church should have the authority to help people solve their problems. My son worked for a home-improvement store that gave superior service to its customers. If a customer approached him and asked where to find an item, he was not allowed to point out the direction to them. Instead, he was to take them to the place where the item was located.

Years ago when our children were just babies, my wife and I visited Community Bible Church. On entering the building and being greeted, two people walked us to the nursery. After introducing us to the nursery workers and taking care of our children, they took us to their Sunday school class and sat with us. We have never forgotten that church and have often recommended it to others. They guesterized in a way that met our needs, and we've told their story ever since.

Questions to Ask and Answer

1. Which of the seven areas of guesterizing found in this chapter does your church do well? Not so well?
2. Is everyone in your church a host? If not, how could you use some of the suggestions in this chapter to encourage every attendee to be involved in welcoming newcomers?
3. Use the Check It Out chart found on page 116 to analyze your welcome. What are your church's strengths? What are its weaknesses?

9

FOCUS ON YOUR PROSPECTS

Be kind, for everyone you meet is fighting a great battle.

Philo of Alexandria

As church leaders, we understand that effective follow-up of guests is an important ingredient to our church's growth. Traditionally, churches have followed up with guests when a pastor or calling team makes a personal visit in the new person's home. Today many churches are finding that this method is no longer as effective as it used to be. A new revolution of church ministry is taking place that is not likely to stop any time soon. We are in the midst of a transition and we are not quite sure where it is going to end up. We need to rethink all aspects of church ministry, even what we call visitor, or rather *guest*, follow-up.

Suspects or Prospects

Church ministry is changing more today than it has in the last few hundred years. In our unusually faddish era, ministries come and go. Programs that worked a few years ago may not work well today. At best a newly designed ministry has an effective life span of about three to five years. After that it will need to be revamped or, in some cases, totally scrapped for an entirely new approach. What remains constant during this period of rapid change is our relationship with people. Churches that hope to connect with guests beyond the first visit focus on serving people well. Such superior service begins with excellent follow-up of our guests.

When we think about service to guests, we make a mistake if we consider them all the same. Minimally guests may be divided into two types: suspects and prospects. Suspects are people who visit our church, and we suspect that they might be interested in the things of the Lord, but they are actually just looking. Prospects are people who attend our church, and we know for certain that they are interested in spiritual things. They are people who are sincerely seeking a relationship with Christ and the church.

This kind of differentiation first dawned on me when I was working as a salesman in a home-furnishing store. Since I was working on commission, it did not make sense for me to spend time with people who were just window-shopping (suspects). Thus I became adept at picking out the shoppers who were going to buy. It really is quite easy. If a man walks into a store with a checkbook in his back pocket, he is likely to be a prospect. A woman who comes into a store carrying the store's recent ad from the newspaper is certainly a prospect.

A salesman's income depends on being able to spot and serve the prospects rather than the suspects. A church's effective follow-up plan depends on being able to separate the suspects from the true prospects who visit the worship service. In general, first-time guests are suspects. They may be interested in the Lord. They may be interested in the church, but then again, maybe not. Guests who return for additional visits are the prospects. By attending your church again, they are in effect saying that they liked what they found the first time. They are back for a closer look.

A Four-Step Plan

The most effective retention of guests occurs when follow-up is focused on prospects rather than suspects. Church growth studies have found that the average growing church in the United States keeps 16 percent of all first-time guests. In contrast, the average church keeps 85 percent of its second-time guests! Thus a follow-up plan must focus on helping first-time guests return for a second visit.

Effective retention of guests also occurs when follow-up is focused on building relationships. Many churches use an institutional approach to follow-up. They focus on what the church needs rather than on caring for the visitor. It is important for guests to perceive that the church is interested in them and their

FIVE PRINCIPLES OF FOLLOW-UP

Follow-up is most effective when guests receive . . .

1. *A friendly contact*—Offer your friendship. Take care not to offend new people.

2. *A personal contact*—Focus on the guest's interests and needs. Nothing takes the place of personal touch in our lonely world.

3. *A prompt contact*—Contact guests within twenty-four hours. The longer the time between their visit and a contact, the less effective the results.

4. *A nonthreatening contact*—Put the guest at ease. Guests have a natural uneasiness about new places and people.

5. *A continual contact*—Follow-up is a process, not an event. A onetime contact is not enough to be effective in our present environment.

needs. Today's guests want their visit acknowledged but are not expecting a visit from the pastor. Churches located in cities and in high-tech and crime-ridden areas will find that people in the community do not want someone showing up on their doorstep without an appointment. Non-Christians and those who find the church threatening wish to remain somewhat anonymous, but they don't want to be ignored.

Step One: Acknowledgment

After a guest's first visit to your church, a call should be made thanking him or her for attending your services. The person calling does not have to be a pastor, but it should be a person with a friendly phone voice. Shut-ins or elderly people may find this a place for ministry. Call Sunday afternoon if possible but no later than Monday evening.

Calling all guests within twenty-four to forty-eight hours shows you care about them and begins to cement your relationship with them. Surveys among businesses found that customers who are called rank the company's service 20 percent higher than those who are not called.[1] In most cases, a phone call to church guests has as much impact as a personal visit.

If your guests are willing, another excellent way to communicate your desire to serve them, and find out important information, is to interview them over the phone. Present your interview in such a way that your guests can choose whether or not to participate. Always ask your questions politely and never force them to answer. When they do answer, listen to their words, but more important, listen to the tone of their voice and what they do not say. Listening is not just hearing, but it's understanding what your guests think about you. Learning to do this will improve your church's follow-up. (See the sample phone interview at the end of this chapter.)

The conversation with a first-time visitor does not need to be long. Just be sure to do two things. First, thank the person for visiting your church. Second, invite him or her back! If the person is open to talking, ask, "How can we help you?" Find out why the person visited your church. Ask open-ended questions to further understand his or her needs. Then do all that you can to meet the needs.

Open-ended questions call for information. They contain words like *who*, *what*, *where*, *why*, and *how*. Most important, not only will open-ended questions help you understand people, but also they demonstrate your concern and care for people's needs. When a phone call is followed up with a personal letter or email, about 50 percent of those contacted will return to your church for another visit.

Most churches send a personal letter or email to newcomers thanking them for attending church. Further information about the church is often enclosed along with times of services, ministries of interest, and special events. A good letter or email thanks the guests for attending, outlines the times of services, offers general help, and is signed by the senior pastor.

A way this letter could be made even more useful would be to enclose a short questionnaire with a prestamped reply card similar to the one that follows:

We'd like to know . . .

1. What did you enjoy most about attending our church?

2. If you could have changed one thing during your visit, what would it have been?

3. How could our church have served your needs more completely?

Thank you very much.

Your Church Name
Church Logo
Church Slogan

Or, if your church uses an email letter, provide a link to a questionnaire that they can answer online.

While it is important to get the information, it is even more important to underscore the fact that your church really cares about its guests. Asking for their opinion is a good way to point this out without actually stating it.

Use a general mailing list for all onetime guests and potential contacts. Mail brochures, church newsletters, and general information to people on this list. Remember that the purpose of this first step is to get the guest to return for a second visit.

Step Two: Enhancement

After making the phone call or sending the letter or email, wait until the newcomer makes a second visit to your church. By waiting for him or her to visit again, you are allowing the person to determine if he or she is a suspect or a prospect. Those who do not return were just suspects, and it is good you did not spend too much energy focusing on them at this time. Those who return for a second visit are your real prospects and are the people to whom you need to give your attention.

The week following the guest's second visit to your church, express your appreciation for their visiting again. A greeting card, specially designed postcard, or another email note would work well. At this point it is important to let them know that your church has something of value to offer related to their interests or needs. You can expect that four out of five guests who visit your church three times without finding what they are looking for will not be back. Arrange a second phone call or visit from someone in the church who has similar interests or may be able to meet the guests' needs. If they are interested in crafts, sports, or a hobby, have someone who has like interests make a call or visit.

A creative way to enhance service to your guests is to establish a "candy express" team. Once guests have visited your church a second time, send out a team of people to visit their home. The team's purpose is not to visit *in* the home but to leave a gift of candy (candy express), cookies (cookie express), flowers (flower express), or baked bread (bread express). In no case are the members of the team to go into the home, even if invited. They leave the gift as a further thank-you for attending your church. This special thank-you creates good rumors about your church and lets guests know they are appreciated.

In communities where people may be wary of accepting home-made gifts, like baked bread, use wrapped packages of candy or cookies purchased from a local store. The gift does not need to be expensive, but a gift that looks cheap would not be well received. A small box of candy from a well-known quality candy maker is fine. The point is to do something that the guest does not expect. By surprising your guests with an extra special touch, not only do you increase the chance they will come back, but also you provide them with a positive story to share by word of mouth to their friends.

Step Three: Invitation to Dessert

The week following the guest's third visit to your church, contact him or her with an invitation to come, along with other guests, to a dessert time to meet the pastor. Guests enjoy getting some face-to-face time with the person who has preached during the worship services, and a good number are likely to accept the invitation. Schedule the dessert at the church or in the home of the pastor or other church leader. Keep the refreshments light and the dress casual, of course. At the dessert time the pastor should introduce the leaders of the church, tell a little about the church and its vision, and invite questions from the guests. At the end of the dessert time, it is effective if an invitation can be made to attend a Get Acquainted Class starting the following Sunday or weeknight. (See more ideas for the dessert time in the next chapter.)

> The last impression your guests have of your church will stay with them until they return again—if they ever do.

THINK ABOUT IT

Mail further information about your church and its ministries to them. Develop a detailed information piece on your church. This should be different from the one that was mailed after the first visit and should provide additional information concerning your church. If guests have returned for a third visit, you should assume they want to know more about your church. Be prepared to provide detailed information about each ministry. A small brochure for each ministry would be good to have on hand.

Step Four: Commitment

The week immediately following the guest's fourth visit to your church, ask for a modest commitment. You could say, "We've noticed you have been attending on a regular basis. Would you like your name placed in our directory?" This assumes you have a directory that can be changed once every three months or so. Pictorial directories are not good for this. However, a computerized directory that can be updated and printed every three months works very well. Placing newcomers' names in your directory does not overcommit them to your church, nor does it make them members. But it does help them identify with your church in a small way. It helps them begin to think, *This is my church.*

If the person is not a Christian or is a new believer, invite him or her to a new believers' class for orientation to the Christian faith. It is best to use a creative name for the class rather than calling it New Believers' class. Try a name like Understanding What You Believe. The class should teach on topics like salvation, assurance of salvation, and basic Bible doctrines.

If guests are already Christians, invite them to an orientation class. The purpose of this class should be to introduce your church—your purpose, values, philosophy—to the newcomer. Nine out of ten people who take this class will end up as members or regular worshipers in your church. (See the next chapter for more information on the orientation class.)

Many guests will have irregular patterns of attendance. Use the four-step plan whenever the guest returns within a six-month period of time. If it is longer than six months, begin again with step 1 and follow through to the end.

By following the above plan, you will contact the guest up to eight times in a four-week period. These recurring contacts will build a relationship that will lead to many more than 16 percent of your first-time guests remaining as active worshipers. Churches that use this kind of plan are often able to retain nearly 25 percent of their first-time guests.

We should not assume anything. In the final analysis, it does not make any difference how we think guests should be greeted. We must be concerned for what the guest wants, and the only way to know for sure is to ask him or her.

Reaching into the Community

To find out what unchurched people in your neighborhood want in a church, you can survey them in person or by phone. This has become quite popular with church planters as a means to discover what people want. It usually involves just a few questions like these:

1. Do you attend any church?
   If the answer is yes, say "Thank you for your help. Please have a nice day." If the answer is no, go to next question.
2. If you were to attend church, what would you look for?
3. Why don't you attend church?
4. Would you be interested in receiving information from a church that is like the one you described?

We do not need to be church planters to survey the people in our community. What's important is that you get information that helps you understand people's needs. Asking potential guests what they want in a church will help you design a follow-up process that works in your community.

Questions to Ask and Answer

How effective is your present system of follow-up? Find out by filling in the following blanks.

1. A total of _____ first-time guests visited our church during the past twelve months. (Count only those people who live in your ministry area.)
2. A total of _____ new people became members or regular worshipers during the same twelve months.

3. Divide the figure in question 2 by that in 1 to find the percentage of people who became members or regular worshipers.

Based on this percentage, circle the description of your follow-up below.

0% to 8%	poor
9% to 13%	fair
14% to 18%	average
19% to 24%	good
25% or over	excellent

Are you happy with your level of follow-up effectiveness? If not, where would you like to it be? What can you begin to do right now to make it better?

PHONE QUESTIONNAIRE FOR VISITORS

Surveyor: Record the respondent's answers in the spaces provided.

Hello, I'm _____ from _____ Church. Is this _____?

I understand you attended our service Sunday
(*fill in the date the person attended*).

I'm sorry I didn't get a chance to meet you, but I want to thank you for coming. Perhaps next time you come, we will meet.

Do you have the time to help me by answering a few questions about your experience at our church?

(Yes) Great. (Go to survey.)

(No) When would be a good time for me to call back?
(Get a date and time.) I'll be looking forward to talking to you then.

Survey

1. Did you have difficulty locating our church?
   (Yes) What was most difficult? _____

2. Did you have difficulty finding parking?
   (Yes) What was most difficult? _____

3. Were you greeted prior to the service? _____

4. Did you enter from the street or parking lot? _____

5. Did you receive adequate directions prior to the service to find your
   way around the church?
   (No) What directions did you need? _____

6. Did you have any problems finding a seat?
   (Yes) What happened? _____

7. Did you feel welcome?
   (Yes) What made you feel welcome? _____

   (No) What made you feel unwelcome? _____

8. What did you like most about the service? _____

9. What suggestions could you give us to improve the service?
   _____

10. How did you learn about _____ Church?
    _____

11. Do you plan to attend our church again in the near future?
    (No) Do you regularly attend church anywhere?

12. Would you like to know more about _____ Church?

    (Yes) May I arrange a visit with you in your home?
    What time would be convenient? _____
    I'll be looking forward to meeting with you. It's been a pleasure
    talking with you. Thank you very much.

    (No) Okay. Is there anything you'd like to know about our Church?
    May I mail you the information or have someone else call?

    I appreciate your willingness to answer these questions.
    You've been a big help. Thank you very much.

10

BUILD PATHWAYS
OF BELONGING

Newcomers don't come with Velcro already applied. It's up to
the congregation to make them stick.

Calvin Ratz

A number of years ago I accepted a new job at a company that
was good at welcoming its new employees. When I arrived at
my new job, the vice president of the company met me warmly
at the reception desk and personally escorted me to my office.
He told me to take about thirty minutes to get settled, put a few
things in my desk, and then meet him in his office.

When I went to his office, he proceeded to take me on a walking tour of the entire facility. Along the way he introduced me
to every employee from management to mailroom personnel.
He answered any questions that I asked and generally gave me
a superb introduction to the company.

We went to lunch with the president and two other vice presidents of the company. During lunch they casually shared their basic values and philosophies of work. My entire first day was given to meeting people and getting acquainted. Nothing about my particular job assignment was even mentioned until the second day.

What took place on my first day on the job would be beneficial to all newcomers to a church. The vice president who led me throughout the day was building pathways of belonging for me. Churches should do the same for their guests.

The various pathways to belonging help people buy into your church's ministry and, just as important, help some people buy out of it.

Pathways of belonging are strategically designed ministries that assist new people in gaining a sense of being part of your church. In a broad sense, building pathways has been the focus of this entire book. Recognizing that people are living without salvation in Jesus Christ and outside the church, we want to help them walk along a pathway that leads to Christ. The pathway began when they first became aware of your church, which led to their initial visit, then to their feeling well served through your various ministries, and finally to their involvement in the church.

There are, of course, many pathways of belonging. Some happen without much planning. A new person meets someone at your church and they discover a common interest, which draws them together. I saw this take place once when a new person who was visiting my church met another man and they began talking about their love—computers. From that point on, it was quite common to find both of them together discussing some aspect of bits and bytes of computers that the rest of us could not understand. A pathway of belonging had developed quite naturally.

In this chapter we are talking about pathways that lead people beyond the first visit into ownership of your church's vision, values, and ministry. This means helping them understand what the church is all about, meet new people, and become involved.

Staff Reception

A staff reception is held in a room set aside in the church where new guests may come for light refreshments and to meet the pastor or pastoral staff. For the best participation, the room for the reception should be close to the worship center, as well as in the natural flow of traffic. If the reception is held in another building, in a faraway corner, or down a long hallway, few guests will make it to the reception. It is helpful if displays are available in the reception room that highlight the various ministries of the church. Brochures, pamphlets, and other information about the church that guests can take home are also helpful.

An invitation is extended from the pulpit, in the program, and by greeters and others who meet guests throughout the morning. The staff reception is designed to give new people an initial acquaintance with the leaders of the church. The atmosphere should be warm and welcoming with casual conversation. No teaching or lecturing takes place. Newcomers come and go as they desire.

A staff reception for new guests helps people gain some basic knowledge of the church and staff. In smaller churches a staff reception can be offered once a month, while in larger churches it could be a regular Sunday morning event.

The Pastor's Dessert

A good way for a guest to start out on the pathway to belonging is through a pastor's dessert. If there are many guests coming to your church, the pastor should reserve one night a month for this dessert. If your church has few guests, the pastor's dessert can be held every other month or perhaps quarterly.

For the sake of illustration, let's say your pastor designates the third Tuesday of every month for the dessert. On that evening guests are invited to the dessert, which may be held at a home or at the church facility. It begins between 7:00 and 7:30 p.m., giving people time to eat and relax after work for a little while before arriving for dessert.

The purpose for the occasion is to welcome those who have attended the church a minimum of three times. Thus attendance at the dessert is by invitation only. No announcements or invitations are given publicly. Instead, a nicely printed invitation, similar to a wedding invitation, is mailed to each person who has been identified as visiting at least three times. Ask guests to RSVP and to dress casually.

As people arrive, they should be warmly welcomed. After they have finished their dessert, the pastor gives a formal welcome. Then he briefly discusses the mission of the church, its key values, and larger vision for the future. He should introduce the rest of the staff and/or other church leaders who are present. In a small church all leaders may be at the dessert, but in most cases only a few selected leaders will be present. After introducing the staff, the pastor asks the guests to introduce themselves and tell how they first heard about the church. If time permits and people have questions, these can be asked at the end. Before everyone leaves, the pastor extends a personal invitation to the orientation class.

Someone should take careful note of the ways new people say they heard of the church. These statements will let you know how well your ad, mailings, and word-of-mouth advertising are working.

Orientation Class

My son went to work for a home-improvement company, and his first two weeks on the job were spent attending an orientation course. He was given a copy of the company's policy manual and for two weeks was instructed in the culture of that company. Not only was he told the policies of the company, which we might expect, but more important he was instructed in the attitudes and actions the company expected from its employees in serving its customers.

We need to have an orientation course in our churches also. Throughout the years, churches have offered a new members' class. When people wanted to be members, a new members' class told them how to become one. Instructions were given on the differences in denominations, and the church's bylaws were reviewed with special emphasis on the section having to do with church membership. The class assisted people who came from a different denomination to understand the new church and its polity. In most instances, if a person came from the same denomination, he or she bypassed the class.

Though there continues to be a need for a membership class, the purpose of an orientation class is to introduce people to your church culture, rather than stressing membership. Thus everyone must attend. An orientation class encourages people to buy into your church's mission, vision, and values from the beginning. Giving people an in-depth look at your church lets them make a well-informed decision about whether this is the church for them. Some people, having heard your philosophy of ministry, will decide it's not the church for them, and this discovery is important. Ultimately whatever decision people make about staying, everyone hears the same message, and they get started off on the right foot.

The pastor must be the teacher of this class in small churches, but in larger ones a staff member can do the job, following the senior pastor's invitation given at the pastor's dessert function. Since some people in our era do not particularly like the idea of church membership, it is good not to name the class a "new members' class." Find a name that communicates a different value, such as Meet Hope Community Church or How to Belong or Discovery 101. Churches find that four to six hours is enough to get the job done. An orientation class offered on a Saturday morning or afternoon for three to four hours or perhaps an hour on Sunday morning for four to six weeks works well. Experiment with different time schedules until you find the one that seems to work best.

The following should be included in the class:

- a brief history of your church, highlighting your core values
- a review of your church's mission or purpose statement
- a review of your church's philosophy of ministry
- a review of your church's vision and goals for ministry
- small-group discussion to get acquainted with each other and form new friendships
- introduction to the various ministries and how people may serve others through them

- introduction to selected ministry leaders
- information on the next steps for getting involved, including how to become a member

First impressions are lasting, so take extra care to make this class an exciting introduction to your church. It should be fun! Take the class on a tour of the church facilities and make sure they meet the main staff. Once or twice, host the class at a party at someone's home or at a local restaurant. Instead of lecturing all the time, use small groups to help the new people get to know each other and discover their values, philosophies, and anticipated role in the church.

Throughout the class, refer to your church as "our church." If a person begins a question with "Your church" correct him or her in a lighthearted way and have the person start over, saying, "Our church . . ." Help the new people gain ownership from day one.

Small Groups

Gaining ownership in a church takes place as people make friends and participate in a class or group. Of course, being

THE WORST WELCOME

Here's a fun activity that helps newcomers express themselves and alerts you to dangers you can avoid.

In your next orientation class, divide the class members into three or more groups. Ask them to think of the worst experience they can remember when first visiting a church. Have them select a case and embellish it, making it as ugly as can be.

Then, if people are willing, have each group act out their experience as a skit in a fun sort of way. They get to vent their frustration and you get to see what not to do in your church. Once they all finish, ask them to return to their groups and remake the story into a positive one, improving on it in any way possible. Then they perform the good experience in skits.

When they are done, tell them you want your church to be like the good skits. Ask them to help you make the church a place where people have good experiences not poor ones.

137

part of a class or group is a good way to make friends. You may want to consider continuing the orientation class as an ongoing small group or Sunday school class. New people find it easiest to make friends with other new people, so they will probably want to continue to develop friendships that began in the orientation class. Ask the class if they would enjoy continuing on together as a small-group meeting on an evening or on Sunday mornings as their own class. If they desire to do so, you will have established a new class or group and further assisted the new people to gain ownership in your church. You or some other leader in the church may need to lead the group at first. Try, however, to turn the leadership over to someone in the group as soon as possible.

Taste of Small Groups

Participation in a small group is one of the very best ways for guests to make friends and connect with a church. When newcomers do not understand the value of small groups, or perhaps have never been exposed to them, there is a natural anxiety about joining one, especially if a long-term commitment is expected. Taste of Small Groups is a way for churches to en-courage newcomers to join a small group for the first time. It's another pathway for guests to travel as they become connected at a deeper level in your church's ministry.

On the Sunday you choose to offer Taste of Small Groups, set up a number of tables in the back of your church auditorium or some other room fairly close to the auditorium. Each table should be able to seat eight to ten individuals. On each table place a sign indicating the geographical area represented by the table; for example, the sign might have a zip code number or the name of a particular housing track on it.

Trained leaders should be prepared and seated at each table to welcome guests and introduce them to one another. Provide each leader with a small-group roster and a children's puzzle that has eight to ten pieces.

Focus the Sunday's message on the importance of small groups in the life of a church, specifically emphasizing developing friendships. Dismiss the worship service fifteen minutes early, and ask those who are interested in joining a small group to make their way to where the tables are located and sit at the table that has a sign indicating a geographical area near where they live.

After people have been seated around the table and introduced, the leaders briefly share that Taste of Small Groups is a way to discover what small groups are like, without a long-term commitment. Initial commitment is for six weeks, after which everyone will be free to decide to sign up for another twelve weeks or not to remain involved. Group leaders should fill out the small-group rosters on the spot, determine the best time of the week to meet, and give each person or couple one piece of the puzzle. Before dismissing the group, leaders should remind everyone: "If you don't show up, you'll be a piece of the puzzle that is missing!"

Dinner Eights

It may be that the new people will not want to continue the orientation class as a small group or Sunday school class. In that case, you need to be ready to help them move down some additional pathways of belonging. One process that has worked well is what has been termed "dinner eights" or "dinner sixes." Briefly, three or four new couples or individuals agree to alternate hosting a meal at their home. Once each month for three or four months, the group moves from one home to another for a meal. Sharing meals provides opportunities for the people to get to know each other better.

In a smaller church, it often works well to have the pastor or another church leader be one of the couples or individuals along with a new family and a regular church member. This helps the new family get to know church members and feel like they are a part of the church. It's always best if groups can be formed from people with similar interests.

New Believers' Class

There will be some new people who need teaching in the basic doctrines of your church and the Christian faith. Thus a new believers' class is another pathway for some people to follow. The purpose of this class is to teach people the basics of salvation, assurance of salvation, and other beginning aspects of being a disciple of Jesus Christ. Also this class serves to explain the differences in church distinctives that some may have an interest in knowing. Everyone will not need this class, thus it is usually not required of every new person but only those who are new to the Christian faith or have unanswered questions. Participation in this class should be open to anyone who wishes to attend.

Membership Class

Recent studies point out the importance of membership in churches. For example, after researching high-expectation churches, Thom Rainer relates: "When membership does not matter, the members will care little about their levels of commitment."[1]

In a study of Southern Baptist, Presbyterian, Evangelical Free, Wesleyan, and independent community churches, church growth researcher Chuck Lawless found 73 percent had a membership class.[2] And it is most interesting, as his research points out, that more churches are requiring membership classes today than were doing so just eight years ago (up from 18.2 percent of churches in 1997 to 31 percent today). Not only do membership classes provide orientation to church ministry, but they assist potential members to develop relationships within the congregation.

To attract the highest attendance, it is best to stress participation in the membership class rather than membership itself. Once people are in the class, they naturally become interested in the deeper involvement in the church that actual membership includes. The curriculum of a membership class often includes some, if not all, of the following:

- introduction to the mission, vision, and values of the church
- a clear statement of the church's expectations
- overview of the church's beliefs and structure (including denominational affiliation if appropriate)
- review of how one becomes a Christian (evangelism)
- step-by-step instruction on how to become a member
- information on next steps after the membership class — joining a small group, class, or ministry

Placement Interview

A key aspect often found in a church with a solid involvement strategy is the ability to position people in a place of service. The most successful way to recruit new people is through a personal interview process. The orientation class will have introduced people to the various ministries your church offers. Some new people may have taken the initiative to become involved in a ministry on their own. For those who have not, an interview should be scheduled in which their gifts, talents, previous experience, and ministry desires are discovered. Following the interview, a ministry counselor from your church should offer several possibilities of ministry and put them in touch with the director of the ministries they select. A concerted effort to interview and place new people will pay rich dividends.

New people are the easiest to recruit for ministry, since they come into your church with a sense of excitement and a willingness to be involved. Does anyone ever join a church with a bad attitude? Well, occasionally there are bad transfers, but in most cases people who join your church have a great attitude about your church and want to be involved in ministry.

Despite this desire to be involved, the fact remains that competition for people's time and energy has never been as intense as it is today. Work schedules, youth activities, and leisure activities compete head-to-head for people's time. So how can churches get people involved in ministry? One way is to be sensitive to the expectations of those who want to serve.

1. *People expect a personal invitation to participate in ministry.* Once upon a time, a pastor could simply announce a church's need for help from the pulpit, and people would respond. In today's competitive environment, however, people expect a personal invitation to serve.

2. *People expect to be prepared and equipped for ministry assignments.* Invitations to serve must come with the opportunity to receive training for the job. People resist taking positions that they don't know anything about.

3. *People expect follow-up, encouragement, and recognition.* Once a person accepts a new assignment and begins working, he or she looks for regular evaluation and encouragement. People do not like "Lone Ranger roles" with no contact from leaders.

4. *People expect service opportunities that fit their schedules.* People respond to ministry opportunities that provide a choice of times. While they want to serve, their commitment must fit into their already busy schedules. The more choices of time and day you can offer, the greater the chance people will become involved.

5. *People expect that their unique skills and personality will contribute in a meaningful way.* People understand that God has uniquely gifted them, and they desire to use their gifts. Thus the more your church can tie invitations to serve to people's spiritual gifts, the greater the likelihood they will agree to be involved in ministry.

6. *People expect to make a difference in their church, community, and world.* Serving in a significant way is important to people. They make decisions on how to use their time, in part, based on the perceived value of the opportunity. The church has the greatest mission in the world, but leaders must communicate how each ministry opportunity fits into the Great Commission. The more people can see the important value of their role, the more likely they are to serve.

BEYOND THE FIRST VISIT

7. *People expect to build relationships.* After more than thirty years of research through numerous studies of church participation, it is clear that the number one reason people participate in ministry is the friendships they develop through serving. Building teams around the numerous areas of service in your church is a good way to bond people together for fruitful ministry.

8. *People expect to grow spiritually and personally.* Ministry burnout is something to be avoided at all costs. People who agree to serve in your church's ministry want to experience spiritual and personal growth through their service.

9. *People expect to have their personal needs met.* Leaders who oversee ministry workers must be sensitive to the needs of those who serve with them. Leaders must be shepherds not just managers. Caring for workers involves listening to their hurts, problems, and needs. The more you care for your workers, the more they will care for the work.

Effective churches spend more time caring for others than for themselves. This means, among other things, they build pathways of belonging for the new people coming their way. What can you do to encourage your guests to become involved in your church? What pathways are available now that new people may follow to es-

---

EXIT STATEMENT

Mission or purpose statements are found commonly in churches. It is also a good idea to write an exit statement.

Visualize an impartial person standing outside your church asking each person who leaves this question: "How would you describe the treatment you just experienced in this church?"

Write down exactly what you hope their responses would be.

Insight: If you want your guests to feel a certain way after leaving, you can ensure that feeling by the treatment you give them when they're with you.

---

tablish ownership in your church? When you answer these questions carefully and then follow them up with action, you'll find that people develop a loyalty to your church and move beyond the first visit.

Questions to Ask and Answer

1. Which of the pathways noted in this chapter is your church already using?
2. Which pathways appear to be having the best results? Why?
3. What new pathways could your church begin to use in the coming year?

11

Invest in People

I believe we are still here to help men and women to learn to
live as each other's guests.

George Steiner

It was Carthage, North Africa, in AD 252 that the bubonic
plague terrorized the city. Death raced from door to door. The
odor was horrifying. People resisted helping each other for fear
of contracting the disease themselves. However, a local church,
committed to caring for people, made a strategic investment in
the lives of the citizens of Carthage. These people chose to put
their lives on the line for the cause of Christ. They called themselves "*parabolani*"—the risk takers. They followed the courageous model of Epaphroditus in Philippians 2:25–27, and their
loving acts of service impacted an entire city. History records the
decisive fact that Carthage was saved from destruction because
of the risk takers of the church.

Our Lord did not call us to Carthage; instead, he has placed us in our present location for the purpose of giving sacrificial service to those both inside and outside our church today. To be sure, the type of risks we face are different than they were for the church in Carthage, but any church involved seriously in serving others must become risk takers. Spiritual risk is the healthy child of biblical faith. It is the day-to-day, responsible, obedient action of the Christian and the church motivated by the love and grace of God. That's our business as the church and people of God. We honor God by having enough faith to take some risks in the process of investing in people.

Serving others does involve risks. I remember receiving a phone call late at night from a lady in my church who was a risk taker. Bev had been visiting friends and while walking to her car to leave caught sight of a woman sitting on suitcases in front of the house next door. Seeing an opportunity to serve, Bev approached the woman to offer her a ride. As it turned out, the woman's drinking had led to her being kicked out of her house by her family. She had a car but could not drive and had no place to stay. It was at this point that Bev called me for assistance.

We decided the best way to serve the woman was to provide her with a place to stay for the night. I met them and then drove the woman to a local motel, with Bev following behind in her own car. Arriving at the motel, I entered the lobby with the woman at my side and received a very cold reception from the attendant. Apparently he was suspicious about my reason for wanting to rent a room. Fortunately Bev arrived and, with some embarrassment, we explained the situation and were able to rent a room for the woman we were seeking to serve. Looking back at the incident, I was very naive and put my reputation in danger. But Bev was a risk taker and for that evening had made me one too.

A Culture of Service

People do not make fortunes by worrying about the daily direction of the stock market. Fortunes are accrued by people who are convinced of a growing economic future and who buy stocks that will accurately represent that future. Risk is a part of the investment decision. Those who invest well reap huge rewards. Those who make wrong predictions of the future lose. But the biggest losers are often those who fail to take any risk, for while they limit their potential for loss, they also have no chance to reap the rewards.

It is the risk takers who courageously lead their people to serve people in the community as well as each other.

THINK ABOUT IT

One of my friends likes to say that there are three kinds of leaders in the church: risk takers, caretakers, and undertakers. Leaders who are undertakers serve in churches that show great fear of serving others. Leaders who are caretakers take enough risk to serve each other but stop short of going beyond the people of their own church. It is the risk takers who courageously lead their people to serve people in the community as well as each other.

The most challenging risk that leaders often have to take is that of investing the ministry in their people.

Even though we know that the clergy/laity gap is unbiblical, putting into practice the truth that we are all servants of Christ—his ministers—has proved difficult to do. Too many pastors and other church leaders make the mistake of holding their people down, fearing the mistakes they might make if given freedom to serve. I'm always reminded of this difficulty when I try to help church leaders begin a small group ministry in their church. Unfailingly they want to select leaders for their small groups from people who are already too involved in church activities to do a good job. When I suggest they select small-group leaders from people who are not yet involved, their reaction is predictable. They fear the outcomes of placing new people in places of ministry. Letting their fears run wild, they become emotionally blocked from empowering new people with a chance at ministry and end up keeping ministry in the hands of a few trusted leaders.

This is not the case in a church where ministry is everyone's business. In those churches we all become risk takers. Unless everyone in the church assumes responsibility for serving each other, a culture of service dies. Leaders must be risk takers, encouraging every member to bring their actions and behaviors into agreement with what God has made them—ministers of Christ.

Saying Yes!

One of the surest ways to empower people to serve is to champion their ideas. If any church member approaches you with an idea for a ministry, the answer must always be yes! Does this mean your church supports and sanctions every ministry idea a person wishes to attempt? No, it doesn't. But it does mean that you champion each idea in a manner similar to the following.

1. You enthusiastically praise the person for coming up with such an original idea. No matter how dumb you may think the idea is, the fact that he or she has taken the risk to approach you with a creative idea is outstanding. How many

more ideas do you think the person will bring to you if you criticize this one? When you can't praise the idea, at least praise the person for being creative and courageous enough to think of it.

2. Ask the person to find five other people who are willing to team with him or her to help build such a ministry. If the person can recruit others, this will tend to improve the idea. If others aren't recruited, the idea will probably die. When the team has been identified, the person with the idea should come back to you. Doing this has a number of advantages. It empowers the person to begin working on the idea. It requires him or her to define and communicate the vision for ministry well enough to attract others to it. It allows the ministry idea to be confirmed, refined, or rejected by others in the church.

3. When you meet with the team, let them know how enthusiastic you are to learn of their commitment and willingness to serve. Encourage them to think through how the new ministry fits with your mission and direction as a church. They should especially think through how their new idea fits with your church culture.

4. Support the team with all the training they need but encourage them to find their own funding. It is the responsibility of leaders to provide the training for ministry (Eph. 4:11–12) but not necessarily the funding. Placing responsibility for funding the ministry on the team developing it ensures that only ministries with a large enough vision to attract funding will likely be started. This is another way of verifying the appropriateness of the new ministry.

5. Assure the team that the church will support them in every possible way, especially promoting the ministry through your church if they abide by the following guidelines.
   - The new ministry must maintain legal, moral, and ethical integrity.
   - The new ministry must be biblically based and doctrinally in agreement with your church.
   - The leaders of the new ministry must attend your church's ongoing leadership training events.
   - The leaders of the group must report to the church a record of how many people attend their ministry, the parts that are going well, and the difficulties they are experiencing.

Taking the risk to empower people for ministry in this way will take a few years to develop. If your answer in the past has always been no when people approached you about starting a new ministry, it will take a few years to convince them that you are serious. Once you prove to them that you are willing to be a risk taker and allow them to begin their own ministries, people will approach you for encouragement, direction, and training.

In the beginning stages, it is not likely that you will find a large number of people standing in line to discuss a new ministry they want to start. Thus you will need to establish a systematic way to recruit, train, and motivate people to serve.

One by One

Getting people involved in an area of service seems simple: recruit the right people, train them, and keep them motivated. But doing so in practice is extraordinarily difficult, apparently too difficult for many leaders to master. Part of the challenge has been the way we have traditionally recruited people for ministry. Institutional-based recruiting worked well for churches when the United States was a churchgoing culture. Years ago people attended church out of a sense of duty. When the church issued a call for service, people responded because it was the correct thing to do. If there was a need for a third-grade Sunday school teacher, the pastor would announce the need from the pulpit and someone would volunteer to fill the position. In an institutional-based recruitment strategy, the emphasis is placed on the need of the institution more than on the need of the individual who is serving. In the example just mentioned, the emphasis was more on the need of the church for a third-grade teacher than on the need of the individual to serve.

Today an institutional-based recruitment strategy doesn't work as well. Most people no longer attend church out of a sense of duty, nor serve from the same motivation. Instead, in our world today, churches must use a relational-based recruitment strategy, which places more emphasis on the needs of the individual than on the needs of the institution.

The best way to recruit people is to start by serving them and their interests. You will need to recruit people one by one, using an interview approach. Use what is termed a "behavioral" interview, seeking to discover what experience (or behavior) individuals have had involving frequent contact with others. In what ways have they served people before and how did they enjoy it? In addition, get to know the person. What are their gifts, interests, and talents? The object of the interview is not to fill a need at your church but to get to know the individual very well. Once this has been accomplished, then potential ministry opportunities for service may be offered to the person, based on what you discovered during the interview. With as much skill as possible, attempt to match the person with the service opportunity, so there is a good fit. Encourage people to make their own decisions for ministry. Ask them to select a ministry that sounds interesting to them or one for which they have some passion.

You should select people whose personalities are predisposed to provide the kind of service you want to express in your church. A few months ago I was walking through a shopping center when I noticed a sign in a store window. Printed on the sign was a message regarding a job opening. At the bottom, in large letters, was highlighted, "We hire friendly people." The manager of this store had some inside information: it's easier to hire friendly people than to train people to be friendly. It's also easier to recruit people who agree with your church's values than to select those who don't and try to change their values later on. You can't teach people to be nice. You can't just say, "Monday morning, begin caring for others." Caring for and serving others must be in their hearts. Select nice people.

Recruit to a team; never place people in a ministry alone. People serving together in teams respond to ministry opportunities better than those working alone. In time of discouragement, they support one another. At other times they hold each other accountable for fulfilling their calling. People prefer to serve on a team and report to each other rather than to a boss.

Recruit to a project that has a limited time span rather than to a never-ending responsibility. The basic principle is *recruit for the short term and renew for the long term.* Declare war on bureaucracy: keep policies, procedures, and formal control mechanisms to a minimum, relying instead on cultural control and people's commitment to their team to control the ministry.

Train, Train, and Train

In 1968 I began working for Radio Shack. At the time I knew very little about electronics or stereos. Honestly I was surprised to be hired with my limited knowledge but accepted the job when it was offered to me. The manager of the store required that all employees come to work an hour early on Saturdays. I expected that we would be cleaning the store or restocking shelves during that time. I was surprised to find that was not the purpose of the meeting. Instead, every Saturday morning we attended a class, which the manager taught, on basic electronics. It was in this class that I learned all the details about tuners, amplifiers, and speakers so that I could serve our customers well. He taught us the basics of electronics so we could converse intelligently with the more technically minded customers. After a couple of years I learned enough about electronics and store management that I was offered a position as manager of my own store. Before I left for my new position, my manager took me to lunch to celebrate my promotion. I asked him why he had hired me in the first place given my lack of electronic knowledge. He told me, "Gary, I hired you because you have a good attitude. I can teach anyone about electronics, but I can't teach them to get along with people."

The principle is *recruit people for attitude; train people for skills.* Seek a balance between formal and informal training. Formal training should be used only when the ministry position is highly standardized. Otherwise, provide training in a seminar format offered in short bursts or blocks of time. Many people attend seminars or workshops for training in their business and are very comfortable with this style of learning. More informal training can also work well. For example, if you have a person in your church who is excellent at providing care and service, have others work along with this person so that they can be trained informally.

Above all, teach over and over again the mission, values, and philosophies that undergird your style of ministry. People need to understand the whys and wherefores of your strategy. They need to be clear on your church's mission and how their ministry aids in its fulfillment. Don't assume your people know and understand these things; teach them.

Golden Bananas

In every church I've attended, there is a common ritual that follows a meal at the church. After the meal, the pastor stands up and asks for the cooks to come out of the kitchen so the people who have eaten can express their appreciation for the meal. Once the cooks and kitchen help have been coaxed out, the people applaud them. The moral of this story? People are motivated to do what they are rewarded for doing. So be sure you are rewarding those who produce the results you want to see continue and increase. If you want people to serve in the kitchen, then reward them for doing so. If, however, you want them to serve in other ministries, you'd best find a way to applaud them as they serve there.

I've heard of many creative ways to reward people for service well done. My favorite award is the Golden Banana Award. One day at Hewlett-Packard an employee burst into his manager's office with the solution to a problem the group had struggled with for weeks. Realizing the magnitude of the employee's contribution, the manager groped around his desk in a frantic search for something to give the employee to show his gratitude. Finally he grabbed a banana from his lunch and handed it to the employee exclaiming, "Well done!" The Golden Banana Award became one of the company's most prestigious honors for inventiveness.

Serving people is hard emotional labor, often demanding great effort. Rewards give people that extra burst of energy that keeps them serving with a smile. With a little thought, I'm certain you can develop your own Golden Banana Award, which will have meaning for your people. One church I visited handed out the Giant Killer Award, named after the famous battle between David and Goliath. The essence of the award was to thank those who had faced the biggest challenge in ministry and won.

> People who feel they are truly part of something important will desire to be vitally involved.
>
> **THINK ABOUT IT**

The best reward may be simply showing gratitude in a systematic way, thanking people for their service to others. A handwritten memo of appreciation tops them all. At first thought it might not sound like much of a reward, but when someone takes the time to handwrite a letter or note, it means the person really cares.

Of course, motivation comes from a positive culture or environment set in place by leadership. People who feel they are truly part of something important will desire to be vitally involved. The most powerful Golden Banana Award is the knowledge that they're following in the steps of Christ by serving others in a sacrificial way.

Everyone Serves

Ultimately, growing churches seek to empower everyone in the church to serve other people's needs. Tell everyone in your church that if they encounter another person with a need, they should attempt to solve it. If they can't solve it, they should go to someone like their Sunday school teacher or small-group leader. If that person can't solve the problem, they should take it to a pastor or committee chairperson or associate pastor. Then, if they can't solve it, take it to the senior pastor (take it to the senior pastor last). The idea is to encourage people to minister to others. All problems don't need to be taken to the pastor or other church leaders. Give members permission to serve others by solving problems themselves. They can do it, if you give them permission and authority to do so.

The *London Observer* reported a few years ago that a platoon of Chinese soldiers was stationed in the middle of the Gobi Desert at a little place called Quingsha. Their only job was to keep the railroad track clear of blowing sand. No passengers travel by train along the track to Quingsha except for an occasional soldier. The only freight the railroad carried was supplies for the soldiers stationed there. The soldiers' only orders were to maintain the railroad track, and the railroad's only function was to supply the soldiers. Sounds like some churches that have forgotten their primary mission and spend all their energy caring only for themselves.[1]

Questions to Ask and Answer

1. What can you do to help your guests become involved in your church?
2. What entry-level ministry opportunities are available now in which new people may serve in your church?
3. What barriers do new people experience as they attempt to get involved in your church's ministry? How can you begin to remove those barriers?

12

Customize Your Welcome

The experience of a newcomer in a tiny church will differ greatly
from that of a newcomer in a medium sized church and from
that of one new to a very large congregation.

Roy M. Oswald and Speed B. Leas

Over the years my wife and I have attended several different
churches, and in each of them the welcoming process was
quite different. Right after we were married, we began attending a small church. The church averaged about fifty people at
its Sunday morning worship service. People greeted us warmly
before and after the worship service, and the pastor's wife invited
us to lunch at her house. Only later did we discover that this was
a normal practice for the pastor and his family. Each week they
planned on having someone over for lunch. If a guest came to
church, which was not often in their small church, the guest
was invited. When no guests were present at the service, they

invited one of the church families. The second time we attended, one of the leader's families asked us to go to dinner. All of these lunches and dinners provided a personal welcome that we appreciated and that eventually helped us join the church.

A few years later my wife and I moved to a new city and began looking for a church home. One of the churches we visited was quite large, averaging more than one thousand people at worship each week. We never met the pastor face-to-face nor spent any time at lunch or dinner with his family. Greeters met us at the entrance to the church and then escorted us around the church building to Sunday school classes and into the expansive worship auditorium. An information table provided brochures on several church ministries, and we received a letter from the pastor later in the week thanking us for our visit, as well as inviting us to return. Getting involved in the church took place through a formal membership class that newcomers were expected to attend. The organized process for welcoming visitors was quite impressive.

The church we finally settled into was a medium-sized church averaging about two hundred people each Sunday. Two worship services allowed the church to squeeze that many people into the rather small facility. Again we were greeted warmly and were invited to attend a bowling and pizza night with a class of younger married couples. As we developed friendships with people in the class, we gradually found ourselves involved in other church activities and ministry.

Our experience of being welcomed in these churches illustrates the fact that the process of connecting people to a church will vary depending on the size of your congregation. Customizing the process of welcoming based on your congregation's size is a necessary aspect of moving people beyond their first visit.

One Size Doesn't Fit All

A good way of understanding congregations is to see them as either small, medium, or large. Congregations are small if they average between fifteen and two hundred people at their main worship service. Medium churches average between two and four hundred, with larger churches averaging more than four hundred.

Of course, this is a very general way of looking at church size, which is actually much more complicated. For instance, there are different categories of small churches, and even larger churches are often classified as mega (churches over two thousand in attendance) and giga (churches over twenty thousand). However, for most situations it is sufficient to think of small, medium, and large.[1]

Small Churches

Connecting people in smaller churches is directly tied to the role of the pastor and other key leaders. Sometimes called a "family church" or a "pastoral church," smaller congregations rely heavily on the skills of the pastor and other leaders in welcoming guests. The pastor and leaders serve as gatekeepers determining who is allowed into the church family and who is not.

When one is welcomed as a guest in the small church, it has overtones of "marrying into" a family or being "adopted." The gatekeepers of the church must take the lead in welcoming guests, which includes getting to know new people, introducing them to other church members, and most important, communicating to the congregation that the newcomers are accepted into the church. In some small churches the gatekeeping role is played by the oldest, or perhaps longest tenured, couple in the church, who are sometimes referred to as the matriarch and

160

patriarch. Until they accept the newcomer, the guest will be held outside the fellowship and ministry structures of the church.

Because the church is small, guests cannot be anonymous, and they will expect to have personal contact with the pastor. Even in churches that have a strong matriarch or patriarch, the pastor will be involved in almost everything. The pastor's participation in welcoming guests is absolutely necessary. This will not be a problem in smaller churches, but as the church grows beyond 125 people, it will become increasingly difficult for the pastor to provide the attention that guests often expect when visiting.

Often guests in small churches receive the warmest welcome if they already have family members or friends in the church, have a talent or gift that the church needs (like playing a musical instrument), or have a gregarious personality. For most guests, however, finding acceptance in the small church is a long-term process, as it takes time for church members to get to know and accept them.

Medium-Sized Churches

Medium-sized churches are sometimes thought of as "program" churches, because they are organized around programs and ministries. As churches break the two hundred barrier in attendance and move into the medium-sized category, some of the aspects of welcoming guests that were necessary when they were smaller will be carried over. Yet the pastor will increasingly have less and less time to spend directly with newcomers, and the influence of key families will gradually dissipate over time.

In place of one primary fellowship group (the single cell of the small church), medium-sized churches develop several centers of activity. Adult Bible fellowships, Sunday school classes, small groups, women's and men's groups, music teams, sports teams, youth groups, and other gatherings take on the role of attracting and welcoming guests. These subgroups become the primary way new people are connected to the church.

Connecting people in medium-sized churches requires more than just the pastor's or key leader's involvement. A process of helping new people find and connect with one of the church's subgroups will be necessary, and each subgroup must be ready for company and willing to welcome and involve new people.

Large Churches

Large churches are the most complex systems of all. Sometimes referred to as "corporate" or "organizational" churches, they are often quite confusing to the guest. Newcomers sometimes find the large church overwhelming with its many programs, large facilities, and large crowds. Just finding a parking space, the nursery, and the restroom can be quite an experience in some large churches with acres of parking and multiple facilities.

Developing and working practical systems of welcoming guests are necessary to connect people in larger churches. A well-designed and developed system of parking attendants, greeters, information booths, refreshment tables, classes for membership, getting acquainted, and finding a place to serve are all necessary aspects of welcoming guests in larger churches. Without such mundane, workable systems, guests are likely to get lost in the crowd and eventually leave the church in frustration.

Insights to Keep in Mind

With the above understanding of different sizes of churches in mind, consider the following insights to help guests move beyond the first visit in your church.

1. Each size church has its strengths and weaknesses. Smaller churches are strong on relationships but weak in program. Medium-sized churches are strong on programs (like classes) but weak in organizational development. Larger churches are strong in organizational structure but weak in personal relationships.

2. Different size churches need different approaches to welcoming guests effectively. For example, small churches may be enticed to imitate the programs and welcoming systems of large churches. Unfortunately, what works for one size of church may not work well for another size. It is far better to find a church roughly the same size as your church and seek to discover what is working for them as they welcome guests. Your discoveries will be far more transferable to your church than ideas from a church of a different size.

3. When getting ready for company, it is best to focus on your strengths in welcoming guests. Design welcoming systems that fit your church rather than simply borrowing ideas from other churches that may be of a different size. While it will be tempting to focus on and try to improve your weaknesses, it is wiser to build on and use your strengths and let the weaknesses take care of themselves as you grow. For example, one of your church's strengths may be offering a variety of fellowship activities. This strength can be used to help involve newcomers. This is what the church did that invited my wife and me to a bowling and pizza night. Whatever your strength is, use it to welcome new people.

4. Guests carry with them memories from their last church. People who used to be in a smaller church will want a personal relationship with the pastor and will find it disconcerting if this is not possible in a larger church. Guests

163

in a smaller church may desire the multiple offerings of ministry they enjoyed in the larger church they used to attend and be frustrated with the lack of ministry opportunity. This will make the process of welcoming guests difficult, depending on your size. Since it is impossible to be all things to all people, you will need to design your welcoming strategy based on your church's strengths, while recognizing not everyone who visits will stay.

No matter the size of your church, develop ways to help people make friends, find a ministry, and get involved in a class or group. Lyle Schaller notes: "Adult new members who do not become part of a group, accept a leadership role, or become involved in a task during their first year tend to become inactive."[2] The importance of friendships, involvement in groups or classes, and a ministry role or task is true for every size of church. The way friendships are encouraged or people are recruited in ministry roles are often quite different, but the need for each of these aspects is absolutely necessary in each size of church.

Questions to Ask and Answer

1. What size is your church?
2. How does your size impact your desire to help newcomers connect?
3. Based on your size, what are the main aspects of welcoming guests that you need to emphasize?

13

DON'T ASSIMILATE ME

The church is primarily a *people*, not simply a *place* to meet. It is a movement and not an institution. The church lives as a committed community *in* this world, which desperately needs redemption.

Eddie Gibb and Ryan Bolger

A few weeks ago I was talking with a good friend about the way the new so-called Emergent Church goes about assimilating newcomers. He told me he had received an email from a person in his twenties and the email began, "Please! Don't assimilate me."

The plea of this young church attendee and his understanding of assimilation have been conditioned by the movie *Star Trek: First Contact*. In this movie the Borg—a half-organic, half-machine collective—has a sole purpose: to conquer and assimilate all races. Assimilation in the movie means absorbing people into a single form so that no one acts or thinks independently. With this understanding, one can see why this person says, "Please! Don't assimilate me."

Assimilation means recognizing each person's unique gifts, talents, and personality, and helping him or her make friends and find a place to belong and serve.

THINK ABOUT IT

Beyond the First Visit has an assimilation view in mind, but welcoming and connecting guests to our church are not, of course, forms of absorbing newcomers to the point of their losing a sense of personhood or individuality. Rather, assimilation means recognizing each person's unique gifts, talents, and personality, and helping him or her make friends and find a place to belong and serve.

Emerging Churches

Those who attend the new emerging churches in the United States and other countries will most likely need to adapt some of the ideas discussed in *Beyond the First Visit*. Like all younger churches, they look at the world through different lenses than older churches and desire to do ministry differently than those who have gone before them.

Emerging churches, of course, have been seen before. Throughout history God has raised up new church movements to reach new generations of people. John Wesley and the Methodist Church, Chuck Smith and the Calvary Chapels, Bill Hybels and Willow Creek–styled churches, and Rick Warren and Purpose-Driven churches are clear examples of God's renewing work in the church.

Today a new movement, called the Emergent Church, is becoming highly visible. These newer churches are related in two ways:

- They are attempting to deconstruct the Protestant Church, as it relates to modernity, and reconstruct it in a new relationship to postmodernity. These emerging churches are moving beyond simplistic adaptations of old models. In fact, they seek to do away with the old models and employ brand-new approaches to ministry.

- They are, in some measure, a reaction against the Boomer church (megachurch), seeing it as lacking in authenticity and spirituality. Specifically, they reject the rehearsed, slickly presented worship service of the Boomer church. Thus these newer churches seek to employ fresh ideas for spiritual formation that are more organic than those used by Boomer churches.

From a practical perspective, some of the new emerging churches are known for making creative use of art, quietness, poetry, candlelit rooms, unrehearsed service, and various forms of community involvement. Their desire for a realistic and honest sense of community leads many of the emerging churches to reject any adaptation of Boomer church practices.

However, not all emerging churches are formed as radical attempts to correct perceived shortcomings in the Boomer church. There is a difference between Gen X/Y churches and true emerging ones. Gen X/Y churches are just attempts to adapt Boomer models for a younger generation. As such, they are not "radical" in their approaches to ministry. These churches often try to adapt the Purpose-Driven or Seeker-Centered model of church to the tastes of a younger audience.

Emerging churches vary in their expressions. The cultural context, traditions, and theological background serve to make each one slightly different in its expression. Thus there is no unified movement that promotes a specific model of Emergent Church. There are, however, certain characteristics that can be seen in many of these churches.

Distinguishing Characteristics

There are ten characteristic views of the Emergent Church. While not all emerging churches will espouse exactly all of the following views, there is enough similarity among them that these provide a good overview of most Emergent Church values.

1. *They see Jesus and the Sermon on the Mount as central to faith.* Thus social and ethical concerns are just as important to them as spiritual concerns.
2. *They see God's fingerprints everywhere.* Thus there is no secular realm as such, but many, perhaps most, things in the secular realm are considered spiritual.
3. *They see community as more important than church.* Thus community happens first, leading to church; rather than church happening first, leading to community.
4. *They see dialogue as more important than debate.* Thus they focus on building relationships first by stressing similarities, and work on differences after the relationship has been forged.
5. *They see hospitality as central to discipleship.* Thus welcoming others takes place in the secular realm as well as in the church.
6. *They see worship as an authentic encounter with the living God.* Thus prefab worship services are replaced with individual creative expressions.
7. *They see shared leadership as the ideal model.* Thus gifted people are free to lead without constraint in a highly collaborative atmosphere.
8. *They see culture as organic—fluid, shifting, and dynamic.* Thus spirituality, community, and faith must be elastic,

creating an uncharted journey with unexpected detours, but always progressing.

9. *They see spiritual life as holistic.* Thus spiritual growth and expression happen not just in traditional acts of devotion but in all realms and activities of life.

10. *They see church as missional.* Thus they see themselves on a mission from God to transform their world.

Many of the characteristics of the younger emerging churches stress the importance of welcoming newcomers in gracious ways. For example, the stress on community, dialogue, hospitality, and mission as noted in the ten characteristics above, leads these new churches to focus quite naturally on caring for those who visit them. They are also drawn to new ways of ministry and connecting new people to the church.

> Many of the characteristics of the younger emerging churches stress the importance of welcoming newcomers in gracious ways.

Connecting Guests

Emerging churches are passionately linked to Jesus. They see the mission of Jesus as being carried on in their communities, and they believe the way Jesus interacted with his disciples is the model for how community ought to be formed when they gather together as the church.

There is no secular/sacred divide in the minds of emergents. Holistic living leads them to see unity, rather than divisions, between such concepts as natural and supernatural, individual and community, mind and body, and public and private. In their desire to model Jesus, they embrace historical practices of the church as ways to connect ancient and contemporary spirituality. The true measure of spirituality is life transformation, rather than the number of people gathered in a large auditorium.

These and other concepts point to the fact that the emerging generation, and the churches they start, is indeed operating from a different paradigm than that common to the Baby Boom generation.

When it comes to connecting new people to the church, these younger churches dislike mechanistic approaches to welcoming people. Any approach that treats people like items to be processed on an assembly line is rejected. Hence, welcoming people must be organic or natural. The flow of guests into the church takes on a more varied and complex form than in traditional churches. Assimilation, or rather the connecting of guests, takes place through the following means.

Sharing Compelling Stories

Emerging churches reject the use of formulas and simple solutions. The use of simplistic approaches to ministry, such as "The Four Spiritual Laws," "The Roman Road," or the newcomers' class, are not welcomed. Deep sharing of one's personal story through intimate conversations is the preferred model to salvation, as well as assimilation. The key is finding a person with a story to tell, allowing him or her to tell the story to another person who has a story to tell, and then sharing the story of Jesus. Connection happens naturally as newcomers are drawn into personal stories, the story of Jesus, and the story of the church.

Embracing People into the Community

Approaches that look or feel like they serve the institutional church are deplored. Since the church is a community of faith, the relational is highlighted over the institutional. Normally, traditional churches expect newcomers to commit their lives to Christ and be baptized before they are embraced into the community of faith. Emerging churches often turn this around and accept people into the community before they are believers. Thus guests are allowed to serve and participate in church ministry and activities in the hope that they will embrace Christ in the process.

Doing Life Together

Emerging churches sense that advice given without request is rarely accepted, so answers to life's troubling questions are not immediately dispensed as though from a "Bible answer man." Doing life together, or hanging out 24/7, allows life's questions to arise naturally, and guests can see the truth of God's Word internalized in the lives of real people, as well as exegeted from the pulpit. As guests see God's Word lived out authentically in people, they are drawn to become part of the church.

Engaging the Senses

God's propositional truth is valued, but emergents desire to learn truth through all the senses. They find that art, music, poetry, media, Internet, drama, and lots of stories are powerful ways to engage guests and draw them into God's story and the church's story. Newcomers are allowed to use their gifts to share in the story in appropriate ways. Often these natural connections capture their long-term involvement.

Learning Together

Communities of faith are learning environments where fellow learners gather to discover the truth of God's Word. In such a context pastors and other teachers must approach guests as parent-like mentors who have traveled further, rather than as know-it-all Bible teachers. Newcomers are drawn to connect with churches that treat them as fellow travelers.

Talking Their Talk

All new movements create their own particular language of ministry and faith as a way of developing a unique identity. This is happening in the emerging churches. For example, rather than use words like *assimilate, tithe,* and *shepherd,* emerging churches prefer words such as *connect, contribute,* and *care.* To these newer churches, building the kingdom of God is more important than growing a church. They speak of a missional community rather than a local congregation.

Although most of the concepts behind the words are the same, the language distinguishes the new from the old, and guests are drawn to newer language because it tends to communicate emphases and values with which they can relate.

Hitting the Streets

Understanding the basic facts, figures, and outlines of Scripture is not enough in emerging churches. Experiential knowledge that is acquired by seeing God at work in the lives of real people and honest situations is more meaningful. As guests see God's truth evident in people's lives, they are enticed to become part of the church. Thus helping newcomers get involved in the lives of needy people in the larger church community is a powerful way to connect them to the church.

Stressing the Kingdom

No longer do people care only about their particular church or denomination. Today there is a wide concern for the entire church, most often described as the kingdom. Guests join churches that help them catch a vision of, and become involved in, God's total work in the world.

Connecting with History

Simplistic answers to today's tough life questions are out. Depth of theological teaching is back in among emerging churches. Younger guests are connecting with churches that assist them in understanding doctrine and the historical roots of their faith.

Challenging the Culture

Emergents resist a blind acceptance of the predominate culture. They are drawn to churches that provide a biblical critique of the culture. Thus churches that seek to redeem the world as well as individuals will find guests connecting with them.

Needed Adaptations

On one of my recent trips visiting churches, I was fortunate to attend a large, growing congregation on the West Coast of the United States. After parking in the church's expansive new lot, I approached the front door and was greeted by a highly efficient and dedicated group of greeters. In fact, I have never shaken so many hands before in any church I have attended.

It was clear that the church had worked hard at recruiting and training greeters. Each greeter wore a wide armband on which the word "Greeter" appeared brightly. While I applaud their efforts, it occurred to me that many younger generation guests would be put off by the clearly mechanistic nature of the greeting system. It was not natural to shake that many hands. It felt like walking through a gauntlet, which seemed more like a machine than a community of faith.

Most guests in traditional churches appreciate greeters, but being greeted with handshakes at the door of the church may have the opposite effect on many younger guests, actually driving them away.

This is just one example of how assimilation of younger guests into the life of the church must take on a different look in the coming years. The basic principles of welcoming people will remain the same, but the procedures must look and feel more natural.

The language of assimilation must shift from an institutional focus to a relational one. Words like *assimilation* and *incorporation* are out, while *involvement* and *connecting* are in. Greeters must still be recruited and trained, but anything that makes them appear obvious or predictable, like wearing armbands, must disappear. Opportunities for involvement must continue to be presented but never forced. Commitment to the local church needs to be stressed, but only as a part of what God is doing in the larger context of his kingdom.

In short, your church's approach to connecting guests must follow the basic concepts already presented, but when focusing on the younger generations, there must be a measure of adaptation to their values and worldview. More and more, the people who are our guests in the next few years will be from the younger generations.

Questions to Ask and Answer

1. What impact do the characteristics of the emerging generation have on your approach to connecting guests to your church?
2. How do these concepts fit with your current church's values and practices?
3. What challenges do these ideas present to your church and ministry?
4. Which of these concepts do you find troubling? Why?
5. How might you address some of these ideas in your own ministry in the coming years?

14

DESIGN A STRATEGY

He drew a circle that shut me out—
Heretic, rebel, a thing to flout.
But love and I had the wit to win.
We drew a circle that took him in!

Edwin Markham

Whether we are talking about the modern church or the emerging postmodern church, the essential concepts and issues remain the same—newcomers must be welcomed, connected, and involved in the life of the church if it is to grow into a healthy community of faith. Normally this takes a planned approach; otherwise newcomers are left on their own to find their way into the numerous relationships and ministries of a church—a most difficult task.

The first step in designing a strategy to welcome guests is to think through the biblical foundation for such a ministry. Along with the short theological sketch presented in the first chapter under the heading "Our Welcoming God," it is wise to look at the Great Commission as a model when getting ready for company.[1]

Christian churches have viewed the Great Commission as the primary motive for mission for years. "Make disciples" is the direct command of Christ to his church, and he added to this command three ways to accomplish it: going, baptizing, and teaching (see Matt. 28:19–20). Thinking about these three methods for making disciples will help you evaluate your total welcoming ministry. Other words can be used and may be helpful in giving shape to your ministry. For example:

Make Disciples

Matthew 28:19–20	Go	Baptize	Teach
Theologically	Salvation	Identification	Sanctification
Programmatically	Evangelism	Assimilation	Education
Personally	Believing	Bonding	Maturing
Popularly	Finding	Keeping	Building
Hospitably	Inviting	Connecting	Involving

Your strategy for welcoming guests should involve the three aspects of inviting, connecting, and involving.

A second step is to understand what guests are seeking as they enter and become involved in your church. The following provides a basic idea of what guests hope to find.

Inviting: A friendly atmosphere
Opportunities to meet new people
Opportunities to make new friends
Opportunities to meet the pastor and leaders
Opportunities to get acquainted with the church
Opportunities for initial entry-level involvement
Connecting: A membership class
Joining the church formally

                Serving in a significant area of ministry

                Opportunities to belong—groups, classes, sports teams, and others

                Giving financially

Involving: Greater ministry involvement

                Growing spiritually

                Learning to use spiritual gifts

                Receiving and mentoring others

A third step is to evaluate your present process for welcoming guests. Take a pad of paper and write *inviting, connecting,* and *involving* down the left side, leaving about ten lines between each word. Think through your church's ministry, making notes under each word explaining how your church invites new people, connects new people, and involves new people for ministry. After you have finished, note your strengths and weaknesses. What is going well? What is not going so well? Use the chart below to get started.

	Ministry in Place	Ministry Needed
Inviting:		
Connecting:		
Involving:		

The fourth step is to design a complete strategy for inviting, connecting, and involving guests. Use the diagram on page 179 to think through this process. Think back over the various chapters in this book. What has impressed you concerning your ministry? What areas of ministry do you need to improve? Use the diagram on page 179 to list the plans that need to take place in the next year.

The diagram on page 180 illustrates how one church developed its welcoming strategy using the Great Commission as a model. Take the rough ideas you developed above and put them into a creative form like that found on the diagram.

Be creative in designing and developing your overview of a complete welcoming ministry. If your plan does not fit the one described above using the Great Commission as a model, develop your own. Recruit a team of people who care for newcomers to help in designing and developing the plan. This is an area in which guests can be of significant assistance. Use the welcoming ministry as a place to involve newcomers in your church, because newcomers:

- know what it is like to be new
- know where the involvement barriers are and can help eliminate them
- want to get involved and will appreciate the opportunity to use their gifts
- want to feel valuable, and their service will make them feel accepted
- are interested in serving

The last step is to begin implementing your plan. After you have designed your plan, put it into action.

List ideas that need to be developed.

Things we already do	New ideas to begin using

Inviting

Connecting

Training

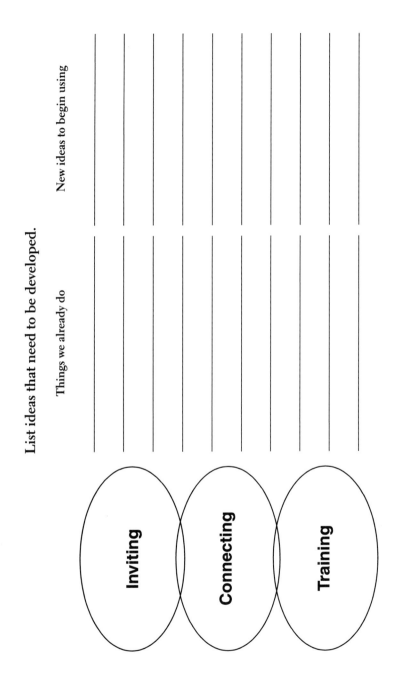

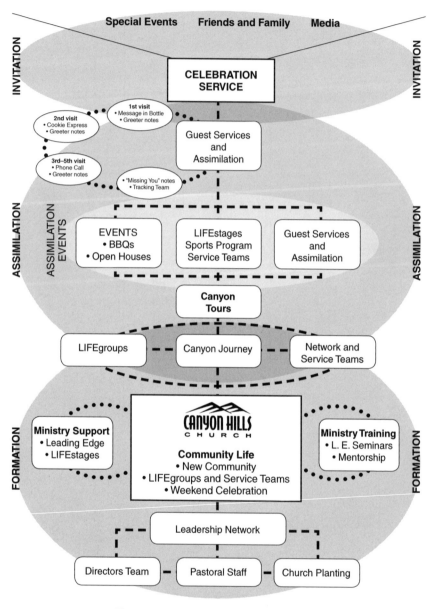

Used by permission of John Reed and Canyon Hills Church.

REVIEW YOUR STRATEGY FOR WELCOMING GUESTS

	Yes	No
1. Our church has an effective way to welcome people, which does not embarrass them.	☐	☐
2. Our church has entry-level places of service available to new people.	☐	☐
3. Our church has an average of seven small groups for every one hundred adults.	☐	☐
4. Our church has regular social activities, especially to help guests make friends.	☐	☐
5. Our church has a way to help guests discover and use their gifts.	☐	☐
6. Our church has a variety of small groups available.	☐	☐
7. Our people care passionately for those outside the church.	☐	☐
8. Our church offers introductory classes for guests—a get-acquainted class or a membership class.	☐	☐
9. Our church has an effective follow-up plan for guests.	☐	☐
10. Our people feel good about the church and often invite newcomers to attend worship services.	☐	☐

Number of yes answers:

    1–3 = Poor—an unbalanced strategy
    4–7 = Good—a strategy that is strong in some areas, weak in others
    8–10 = Excellent—a balanced strategy

Questions to Ask and Answer

1. How well is your welcoming plan working?
2. What welcoming ministries are in place? What needs to be added?
3. What steps are you going to take to build a better welcoming ministry?

NOTES

Chapter 1 Empty the Cat Litter Box

1. Win Arn and Charles Arn, *Who Cares about Love?* (Pasadena: Church Growth, 1986).

Chapter 2 Be a Great Host

1. For a full discussion of front-door and side-door churches, see Daniel R. Reeves and Ron Jensen, *Always Advancing* (San Bernardino, CA: Here's Life Publishers, 1984).

2. See Win Arn, *The Church Growth Ratio Book* (Monrovia, CA: Church Growth, 1990).

3. See Flavil R. Yeakley Jr., *Why Churches Grow* (Nashville: Christian Communications, 1986).

4. See Gary McIntosh and Glen Martin, *Finding Them, Keeping Them* (Nashville: Broadman, 1992).

Chapter 3 See What Visitors See

1. Ron Willingham, *Hey, I'm the Customer* (New Jersey: Prentice Hall, 1992), 9, 11.

2. See Jonathan Gainsbrugh, *Winning the Backdoor War* (Elk Grove, CA, 1993).

Chapter 4 Notch Up Your Ministry

1. Gary McIntosh and Gary Martin, *The Issachar Factor* (Broadman and Holman, 1993), 40.

Chapter 6 Spread the Word

1. Jerry R. Wilson, *Word-of-Mouth Marketing* (New York: John Wiley, 1991), 22.
2. Ibid.

Chapter 7 Start New Ministries

1. See Roy M. Oswald and Speed B. Leas, *The Inviting Church* (Washington, DC: The Alban Institute, 1987).
2. For an excellent resource on starting new ministries, see Robert E. Logan and Larry Short, *Mobilizing for Compassion* (Grand Rapids: Revell, 1994).

Chapter 8 Guesterize Your Church

1. "The Numbers News," *American Demographics* (May 1994).
2. Charles Arn, "Improving Your Welcome," *Church Growth Network* newsletter 14, no. 7 (July 2002): 1.
3. Ibid.
4. Ibid., 2.
5. Ibid.

Chapter 9 Focus on Your Prospects

1. George R. Walther, "Your Secret Opportunity," *Success* (May 1992), 12.

Chapter 10 Build Pathways of Belonging

1. Thom Rainer, quoted in Chuck Lawless, *Membership Matters* (Grand Rapids: Zondervan, 2005), 12.
2. Ibid., 19.

Chapter 11 Invest in People

1. Reported in *Illustration Digest* (June–August, 1993), 14.

Chapter 12 Customize Your Welcome

1. See Gary L. McIntosh, *One Size Doesn't Fit All* (Grand Rapids: Revell, 1999).
2. Lyle E. Schaller, *Assimilating New Members* (Nashville: Abingdon, 1978), 77.

Chapter 14 Design a Strategy

1. See also Patrick R. Keifert, *Welcoming the Stranger: A Public Theology of Worship and Evangelism* (Minneapolis: Fortress Press, 1992).

RECOMMENDED RESOURCES

Arn, Win. *The Church Growth Ratio Book: How to Have a Revitalized, Healthy, Growing, Loving Church*. Monrovia, CA: Church Growth, 1990.

Arn, Win, Carroll Nyquist, and Charles Arn. *Who Cares about Love? How to Bring Together the Great Commission and the Great Commandment*. Pasadena, CA: Church Growth, 1986.

Gainsbrugh, Jonathan. *Winning the Backdoor War: Growing Your Church by Closing Its Seven Backdoors*. Elkgrove, CA: 1993.

Harre, Alan F. *Close the Backdoor: Ways to Create a Caring Congregational Fellowship*. St. Louis, MO: Concordia, 1984.

Keifert, Patrick R. *Welcoming the Stranger: A Public Theology of Worship and Evangelism*. Minneapolis: Fortress, 1992.

Lawless, Chuck. *Membership Matters*. Grand Rapids: Zondervan, 2005.

Logan, Robert E., and Larry Short. *Mobilizing for Compassion*. Grand Rapids: Revell, 1994.

Mann, Alice B. *Incorporation of New Members in the Episcopal Church: A Manual for Clergy and Lay Leaders*. Philadelphia: Ascension Press, 1983.

McIntosh, Gary L. *What Visitors See* video. Available from Church Growth Network, P.O. Box 892589, Temecula, CA 92589. 1-951-506-9086.

Mead, Loren B. *More Than Numbers: The Ways Churches Grow*. Bethesda, MD: The Alban Institute, 1993.

Oswald, Roy M., and Speed B. Leas. *The Inviting Church: A Study of New Member Assimilation*. Washington, DC: The Alban Institute, 1987.

Reeves, Daniel R., and Ron Jensen. *Always Advancing*. San Bernardino, CA: Here's Life Publishers, 1984.

Schaller, Lyle E. *Assimilating New Members*. Nashville: Abingdon, 1978.

Stevens, Tim, and Tony Morgan. *Simply Strategic Growth: Attracting a Crowd to Your Church*. Loveland, CO: Group, 2005.

———. *Simply Strategic Volunteers: Empowering People for Ministry*. Loveland, CO: Group, 2005.

Weeks, Andrew D. *Welcome! Tools and Techniques for New Member Ministry*. Washington, DC: The Alban Institute, 1992.

Wilson, Marlene. *How to Mobilize Church Volunteers*. Minneapolis: Augsburg, 1983.

Yeakley, Flavil R., Jr. *Why Churches Grow*. 3rd. ed. Nashville: Christian Communications, 1986.

ABOUT THE AUTHOR

Gary L. McIntosh, D.Min., Ph.D., is a nationally known author, speaker, educator, and consultant. He serves as professor of Christian ministry and leadership at Talbot School of Theology, Biola University, in La Mirada, California, and has written extensively in the field of pastoral ministry, leadership, generational studies, and church growth.

As president of The Church Growth Network, a church consulting firm he founded in 1989, Dr. McIntosh has served more than one thousand churches in fifty-eight denominations throughout the United States and Canada. The 1995 and 1996 president of the American Society for Church Growth, he edits both the *Growth Points* newsletter and the *Journal of the American Society for Church Growth*.

Services Available

Dr. McIntosh's services include: keynote presentations at major meetings, seminars and workshops, training courses, and ongoing consultation/coaching.

For a live presentation of the material found in *Beyond the First Visit* or to request a catalog of materials or other information on Dr. McIntosh's availability and ministry contact:

Church Growth Network
P.O. Box 892589
Temecula, CA 92589–2589
951-506-3086
Email: cgnet@verizon.net
On the World Wide Web at:
www.churchgrowthnetwork.com

HELP FOR FACING THE CHALLENGES *of* MINISTRY *in the* REAL WORLD.

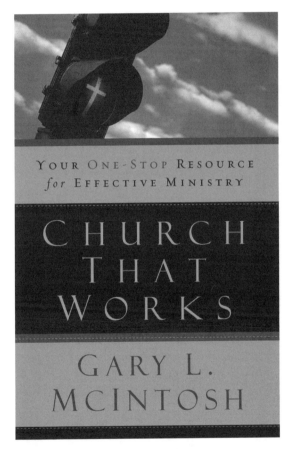

Church That Works offers sound guidance on the ministry details and decisions that sooner or later require your attention. In this idea-packed book you will find practical advice on issues pastors commonly face, such as

- assessing new ministry trends
- welcoming and following up with newcomers to your church
- planning worship services

- revitalizing a declining church
- ministering across generations
- leading and compensating staff

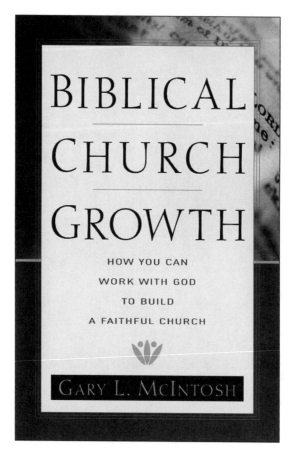